EASY
FLOWER

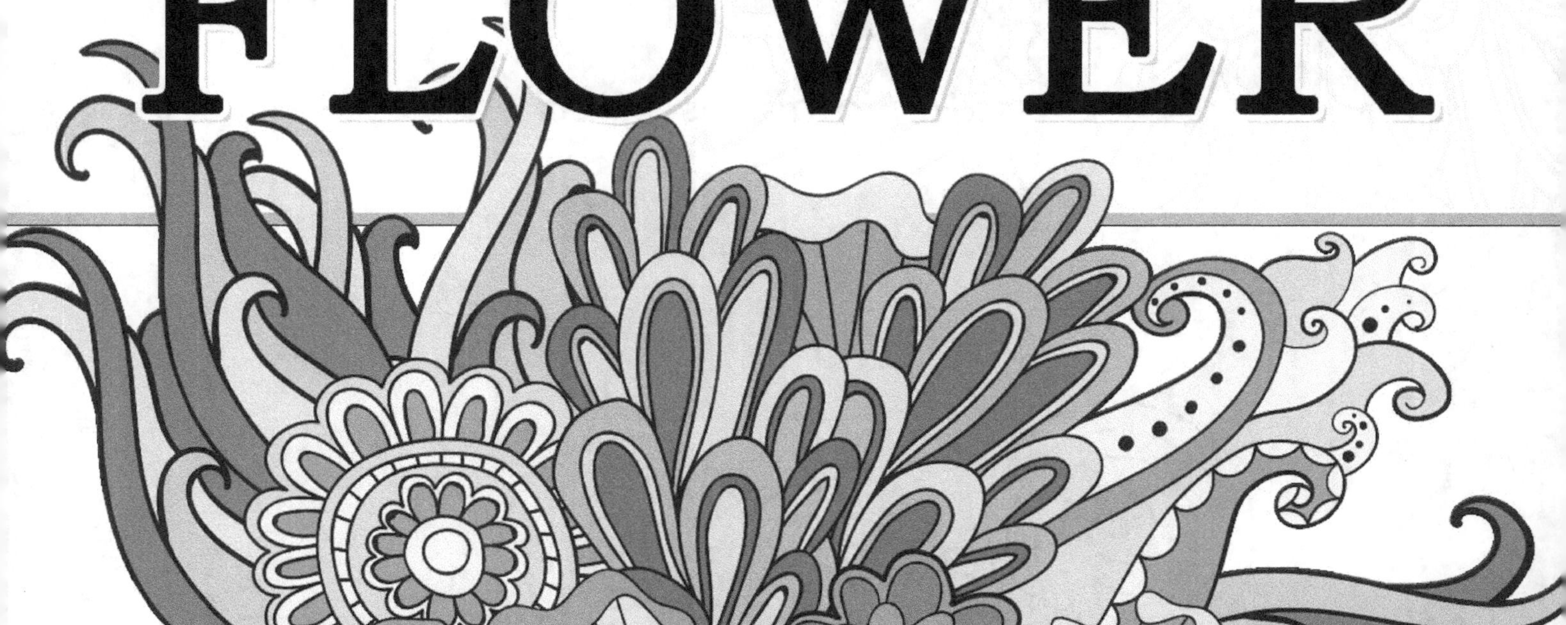

COLORING BOOKS FOR ADULTS

MINDFULNESS AND STRESS RELIEVING PATTERNS

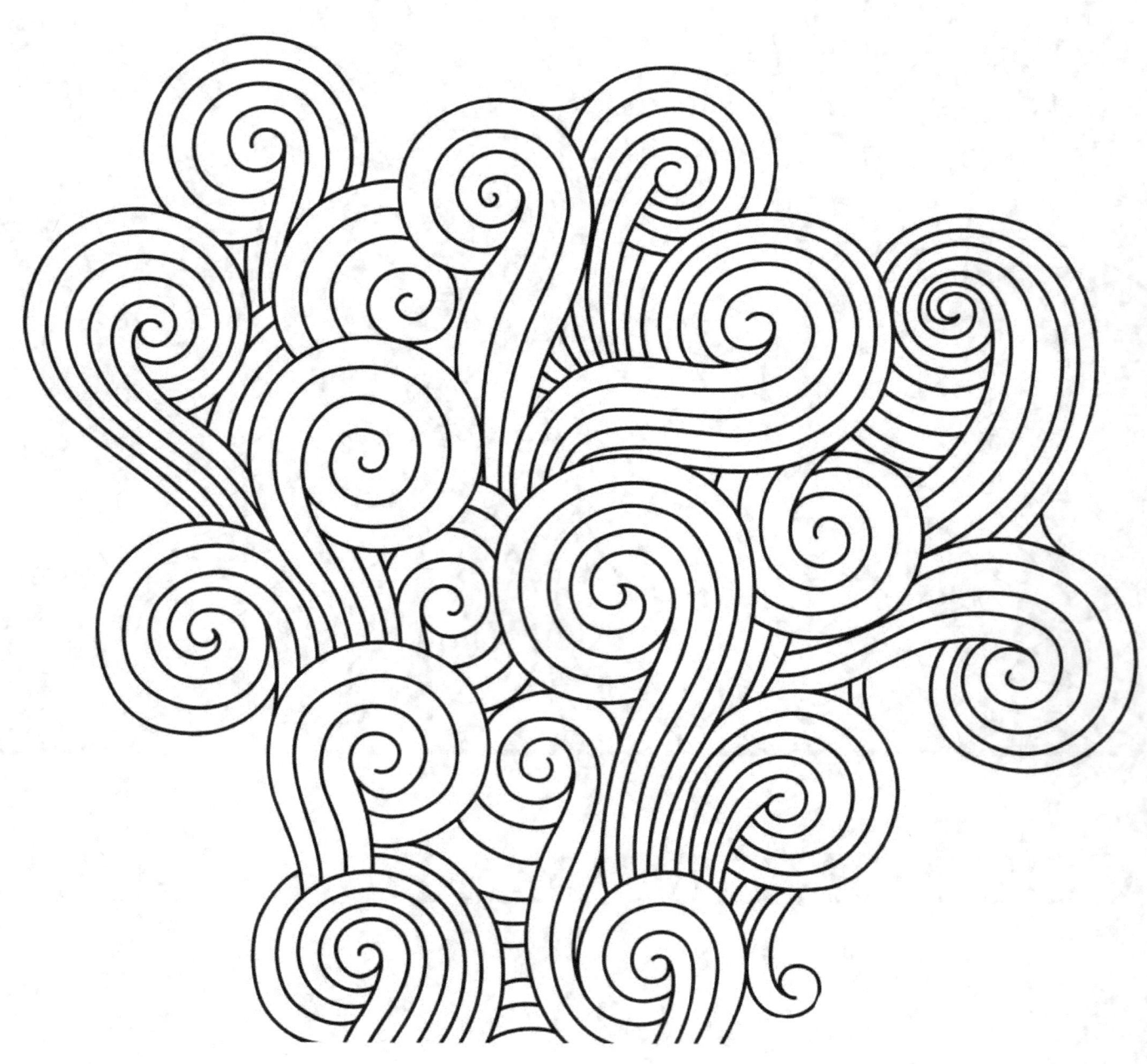

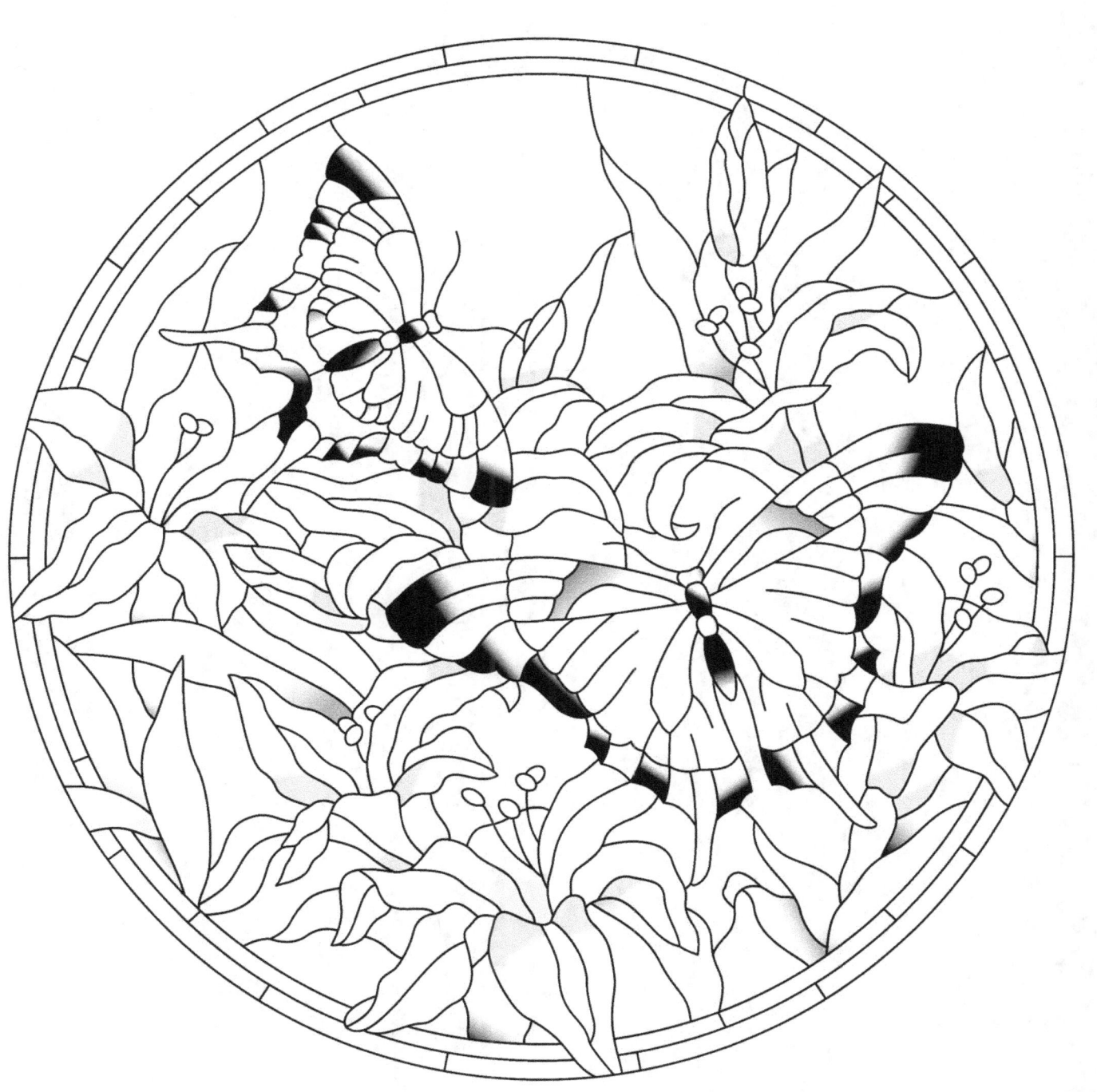

1.

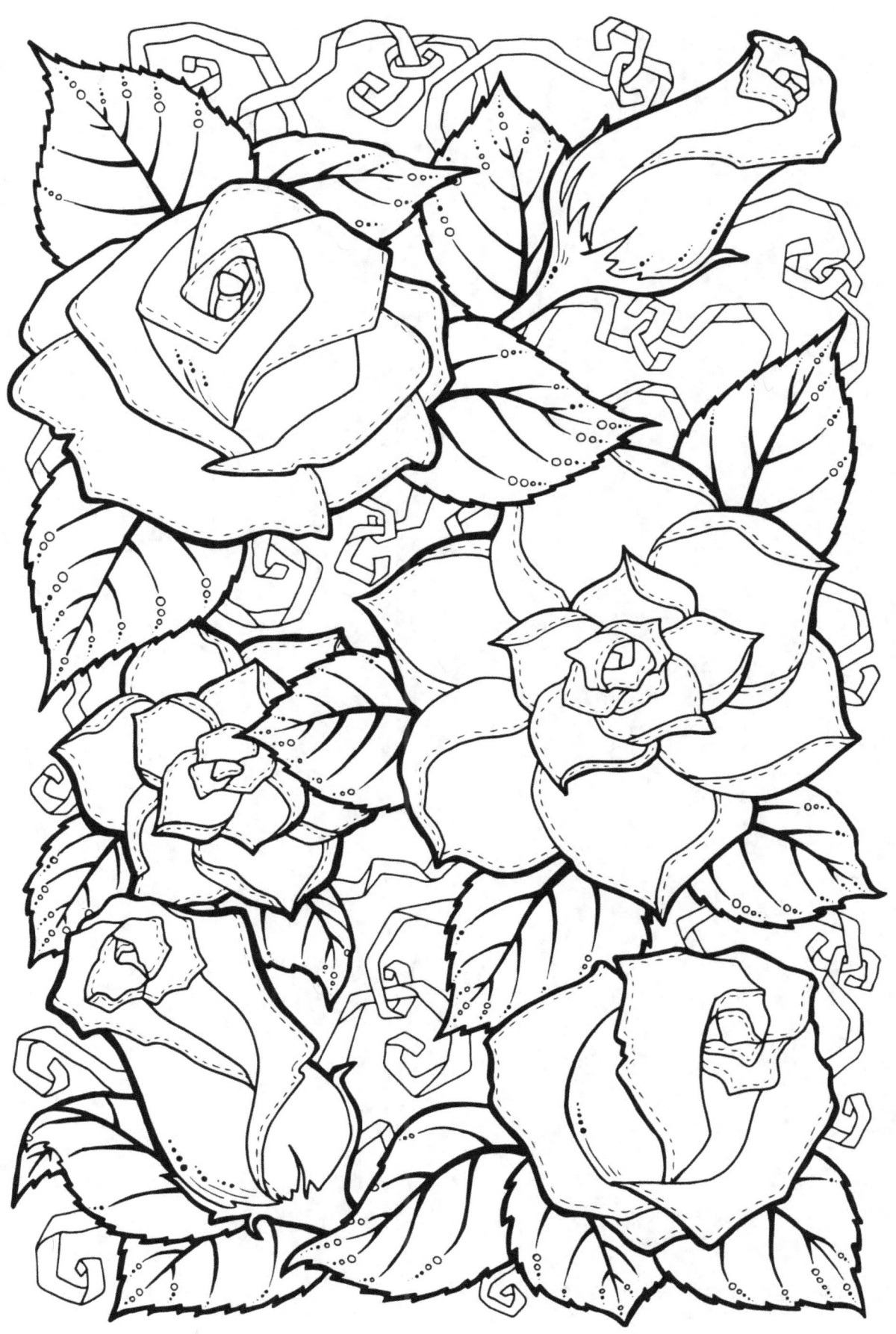

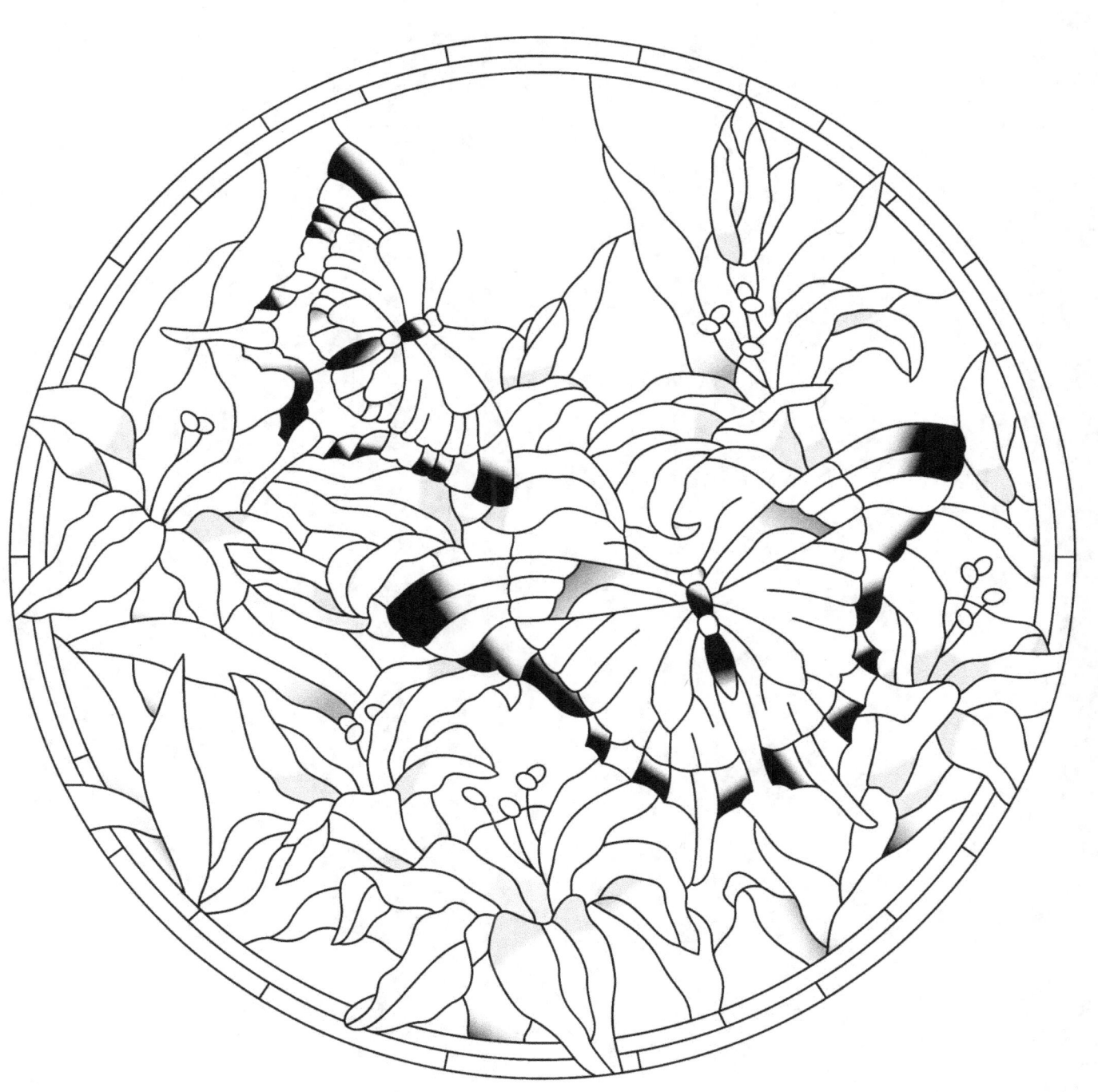

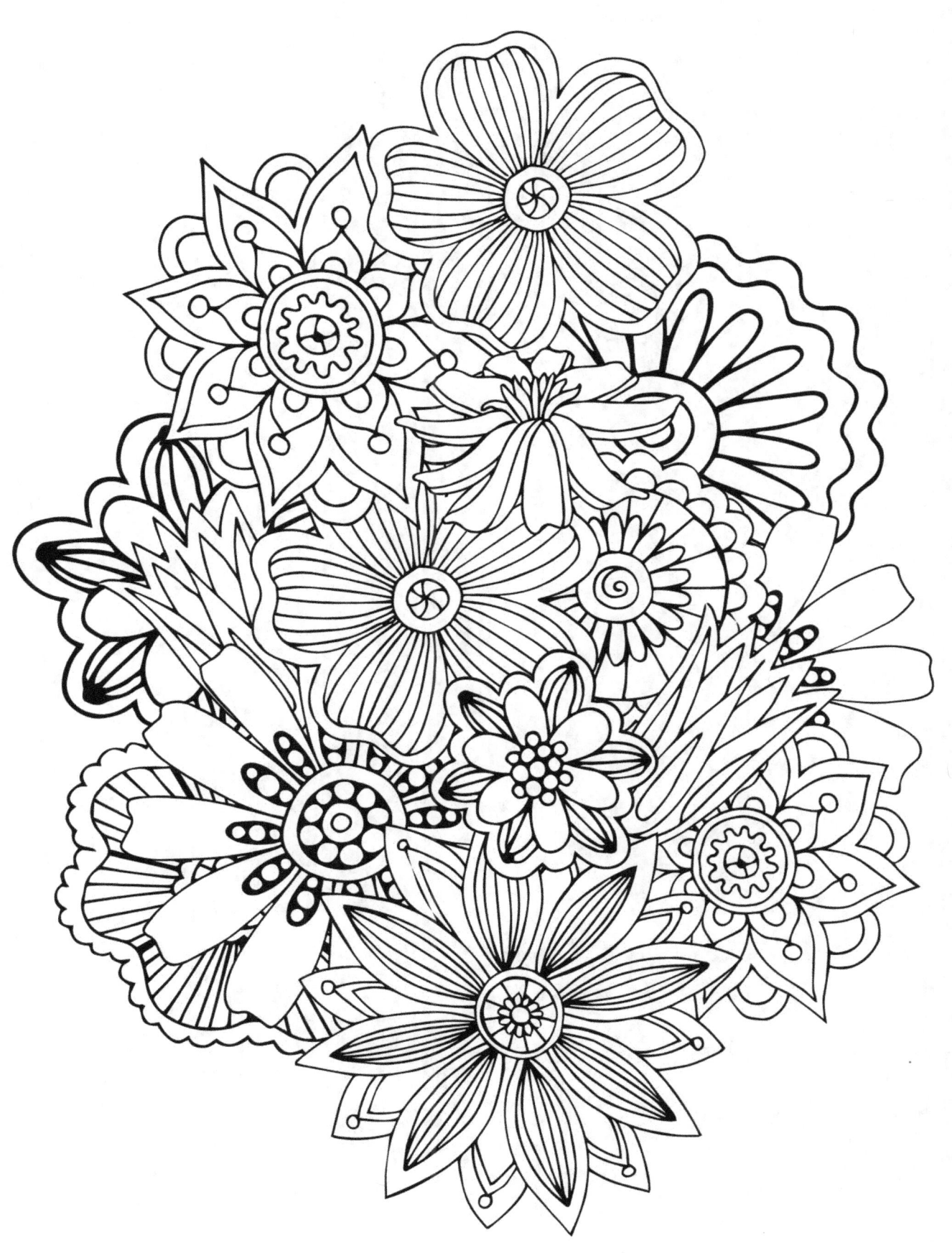

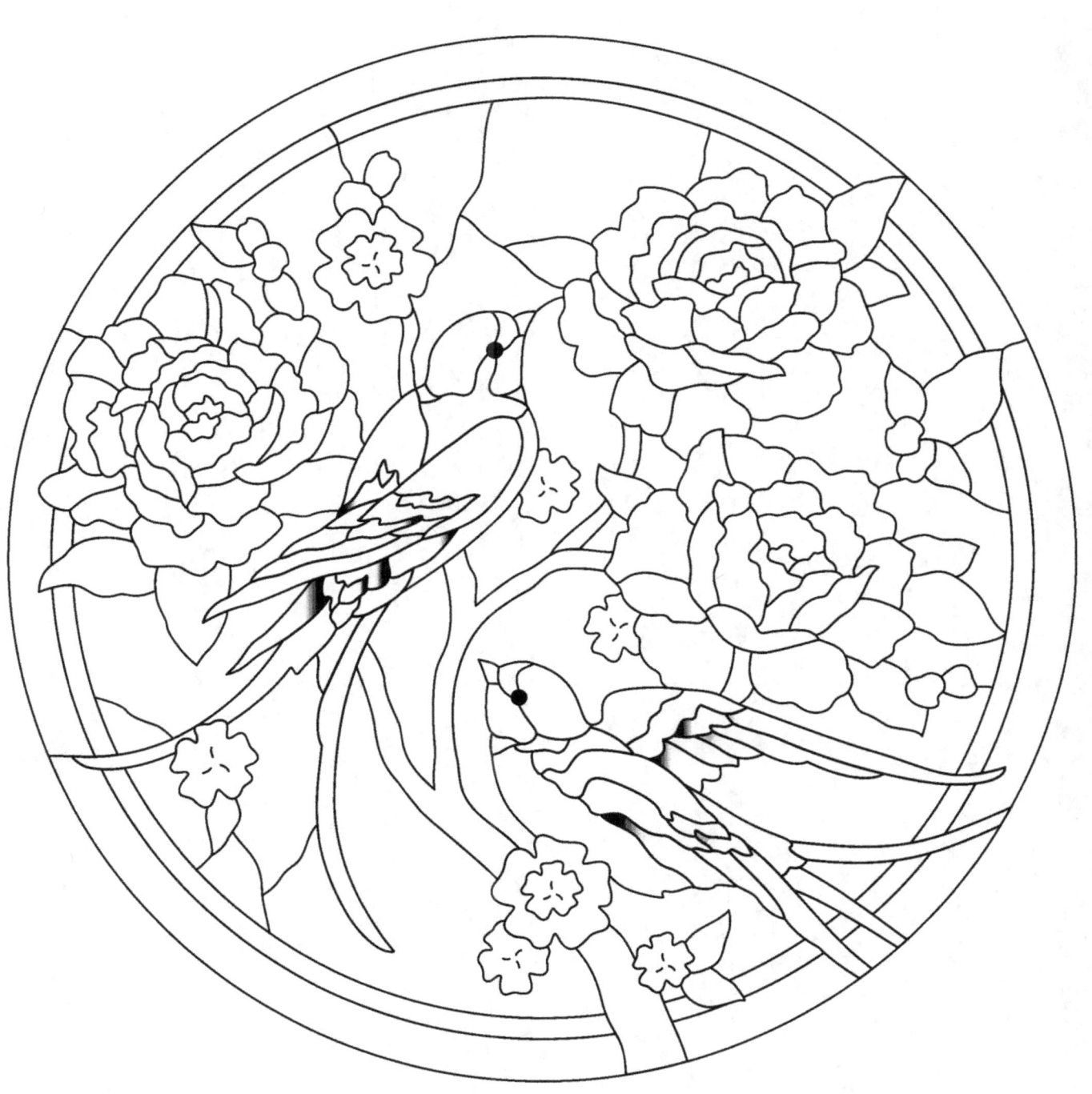

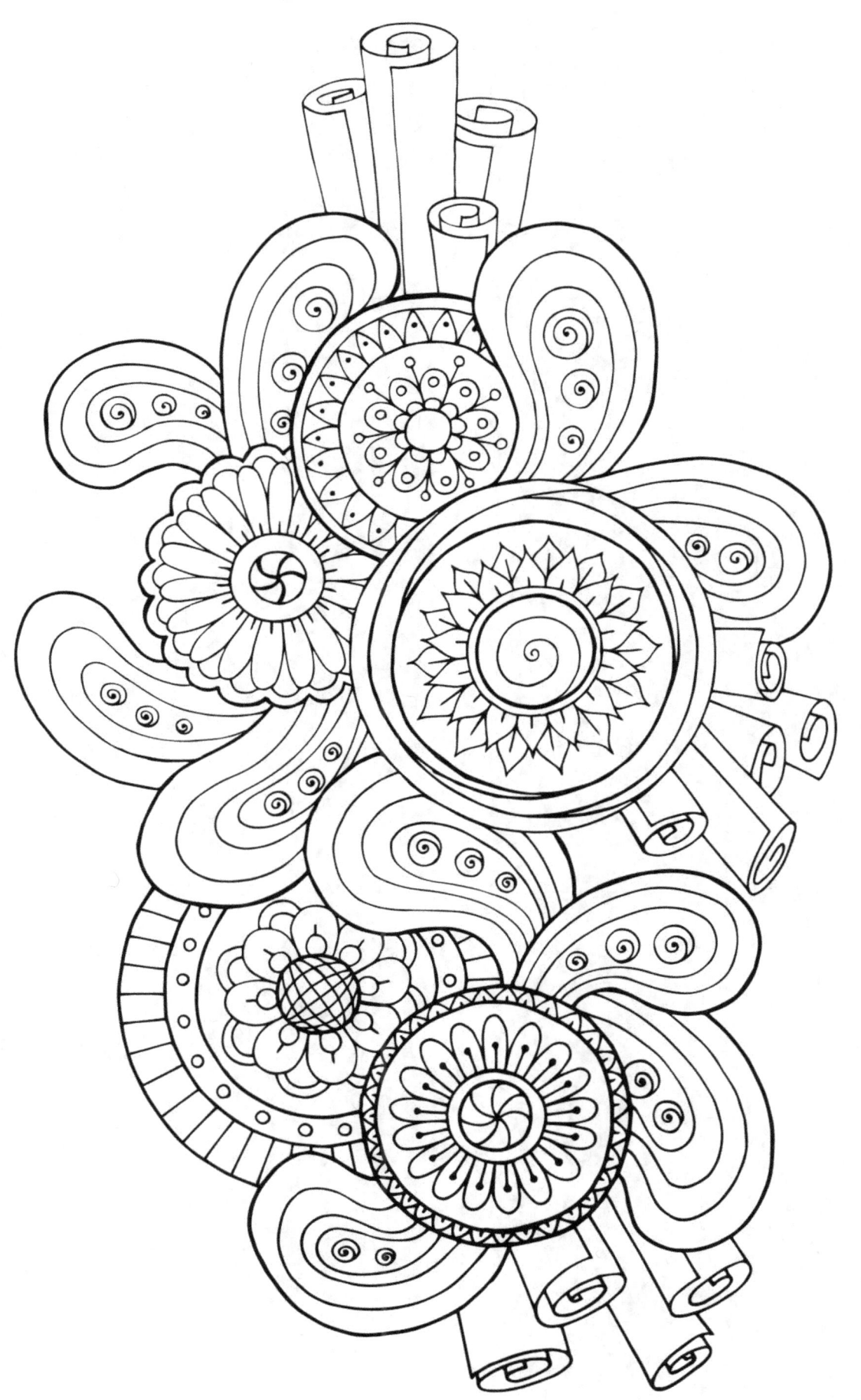

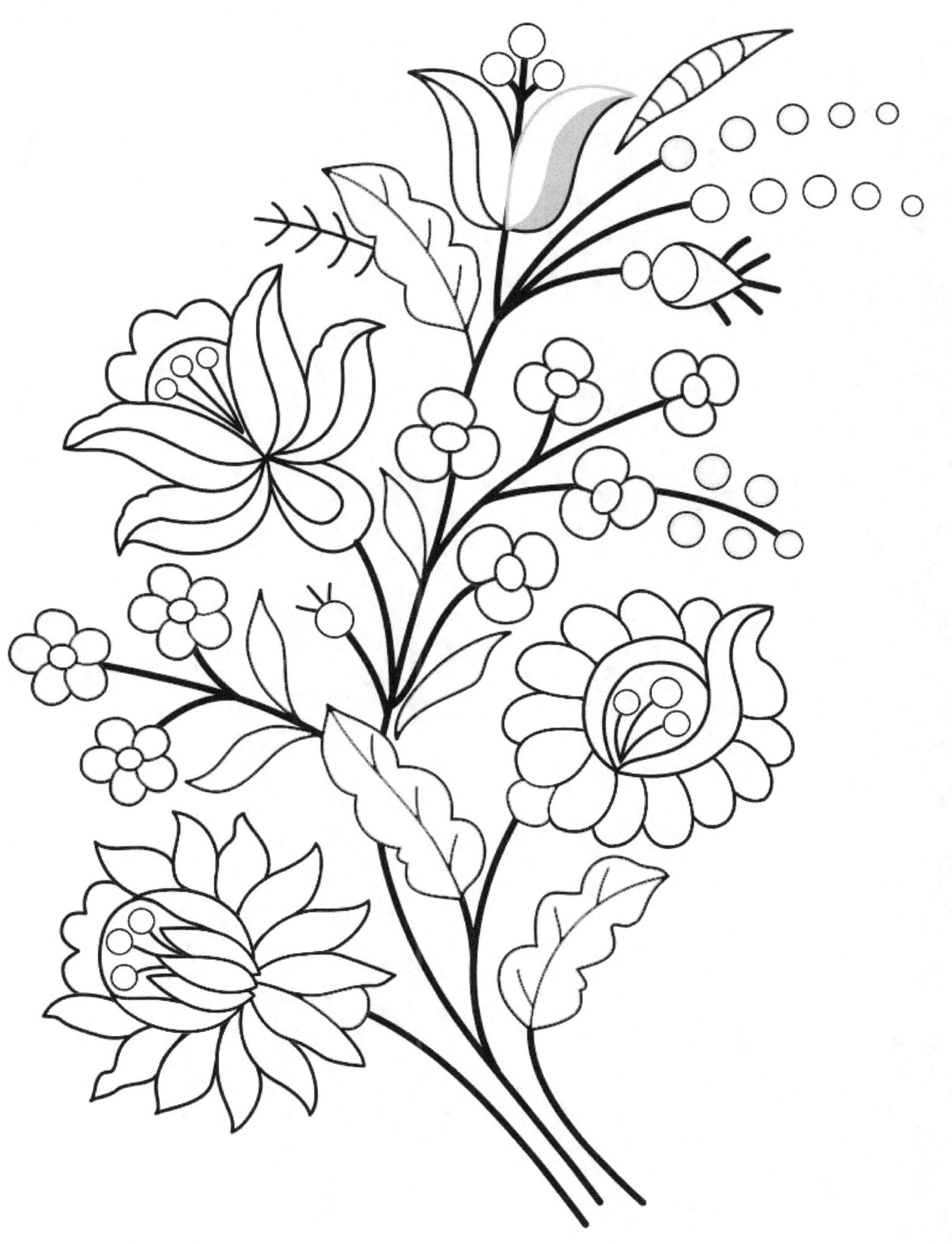

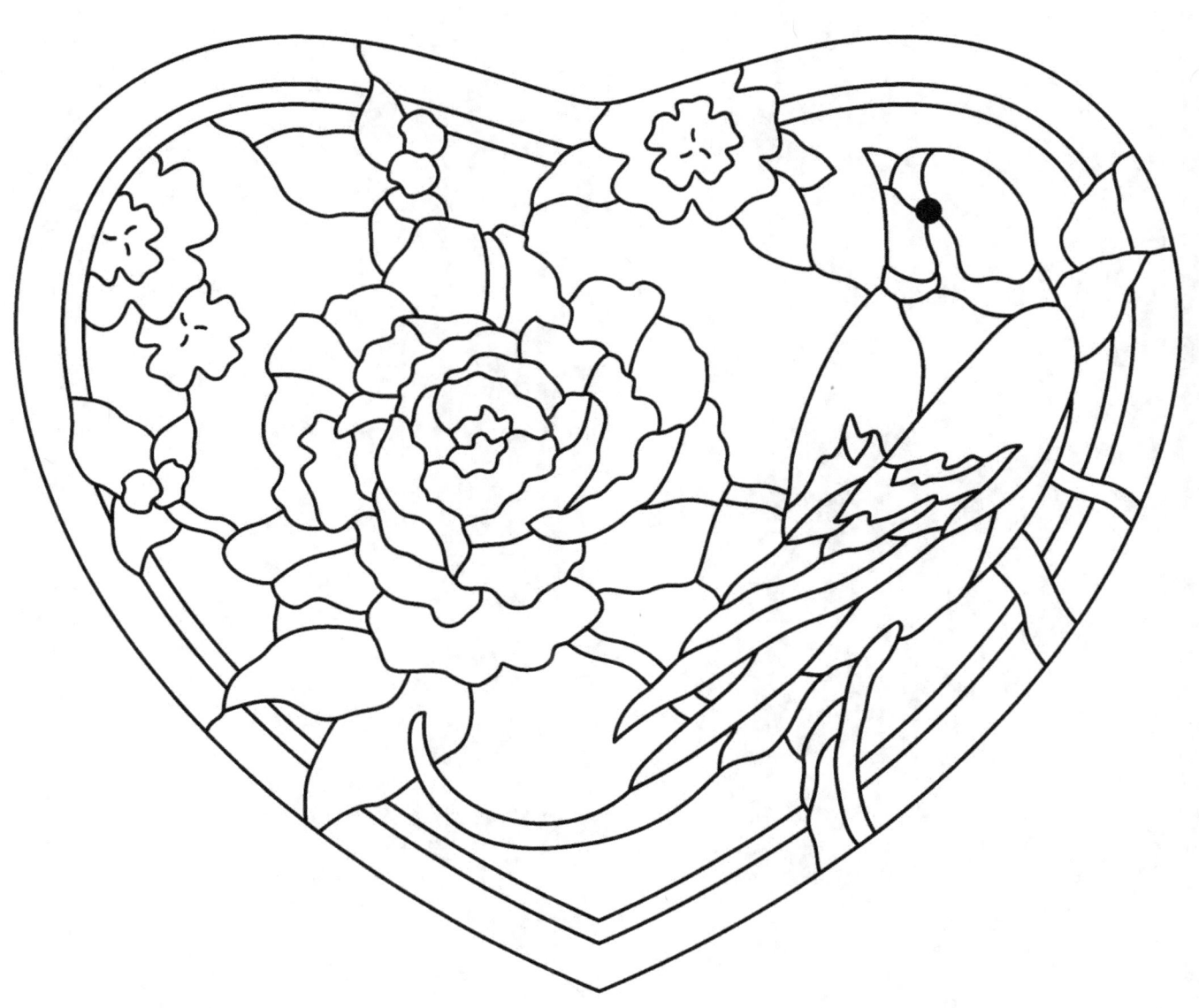

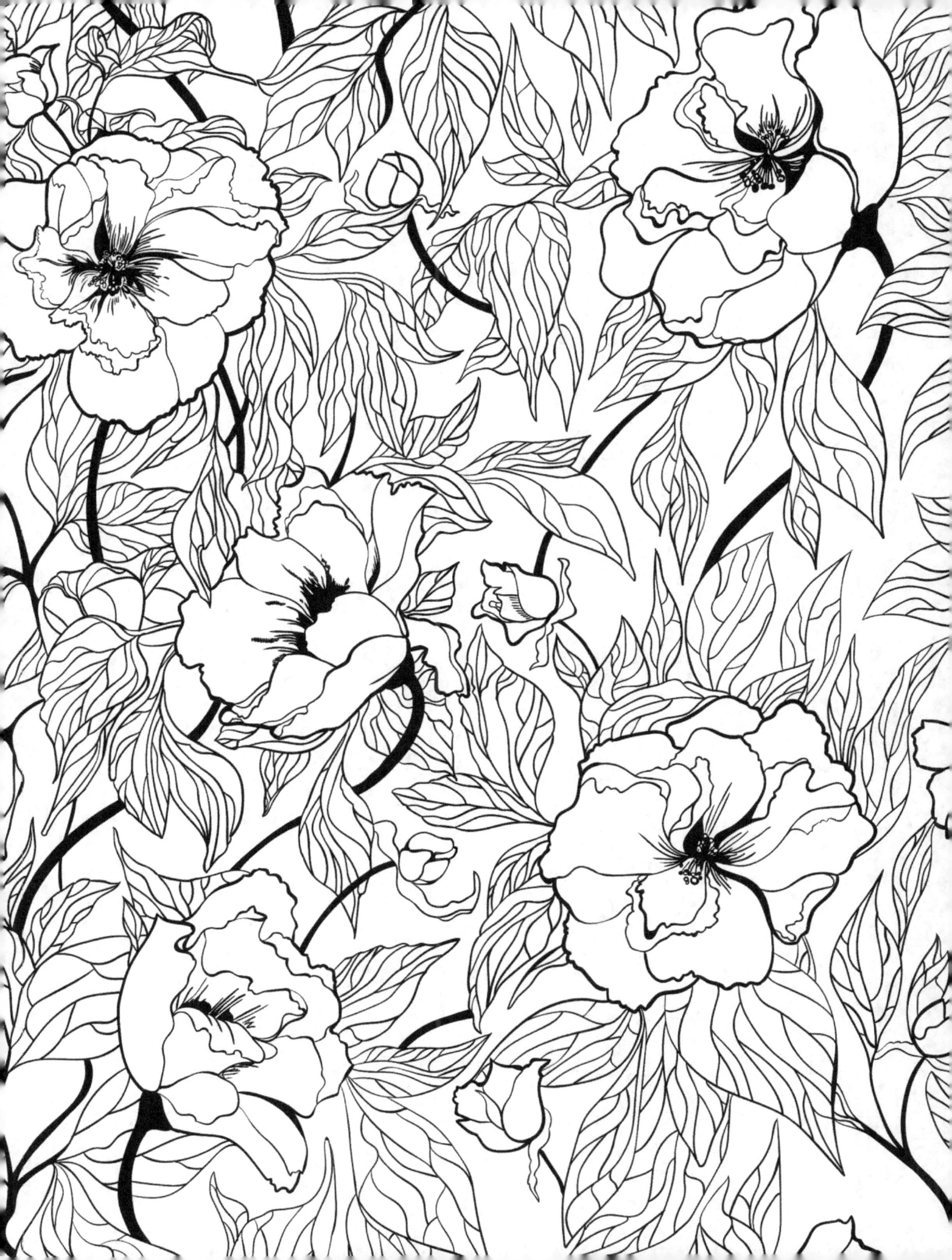

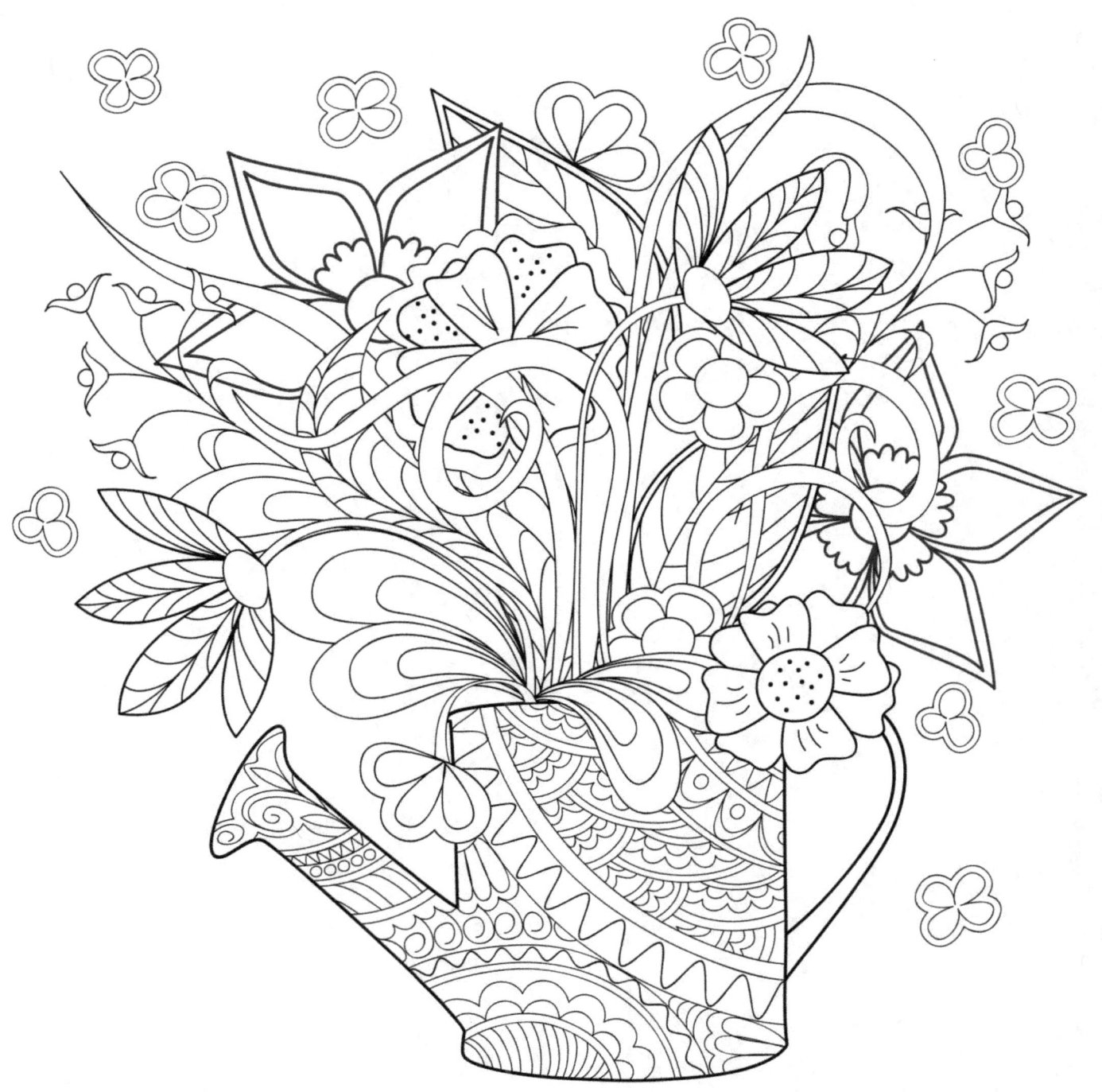

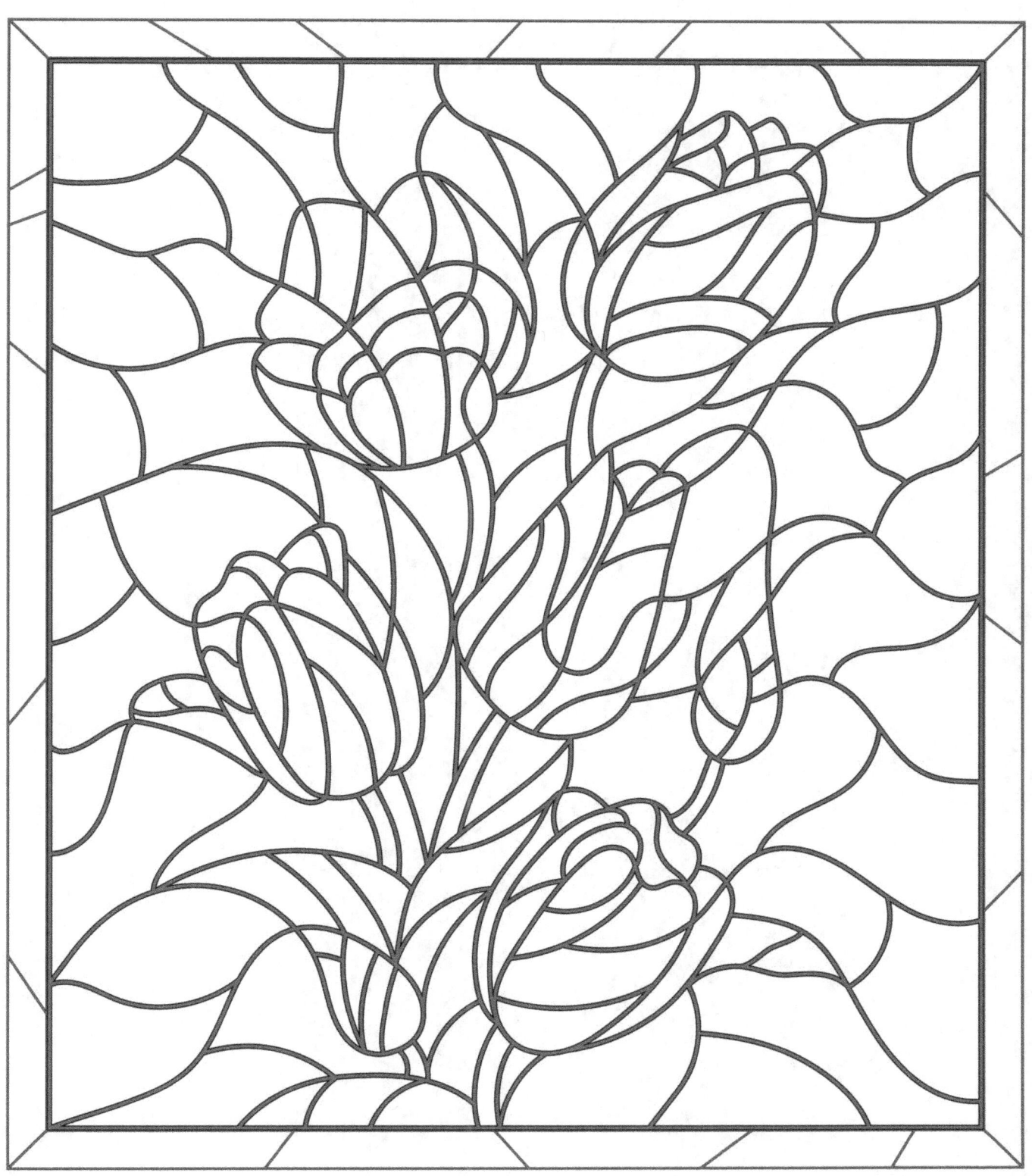

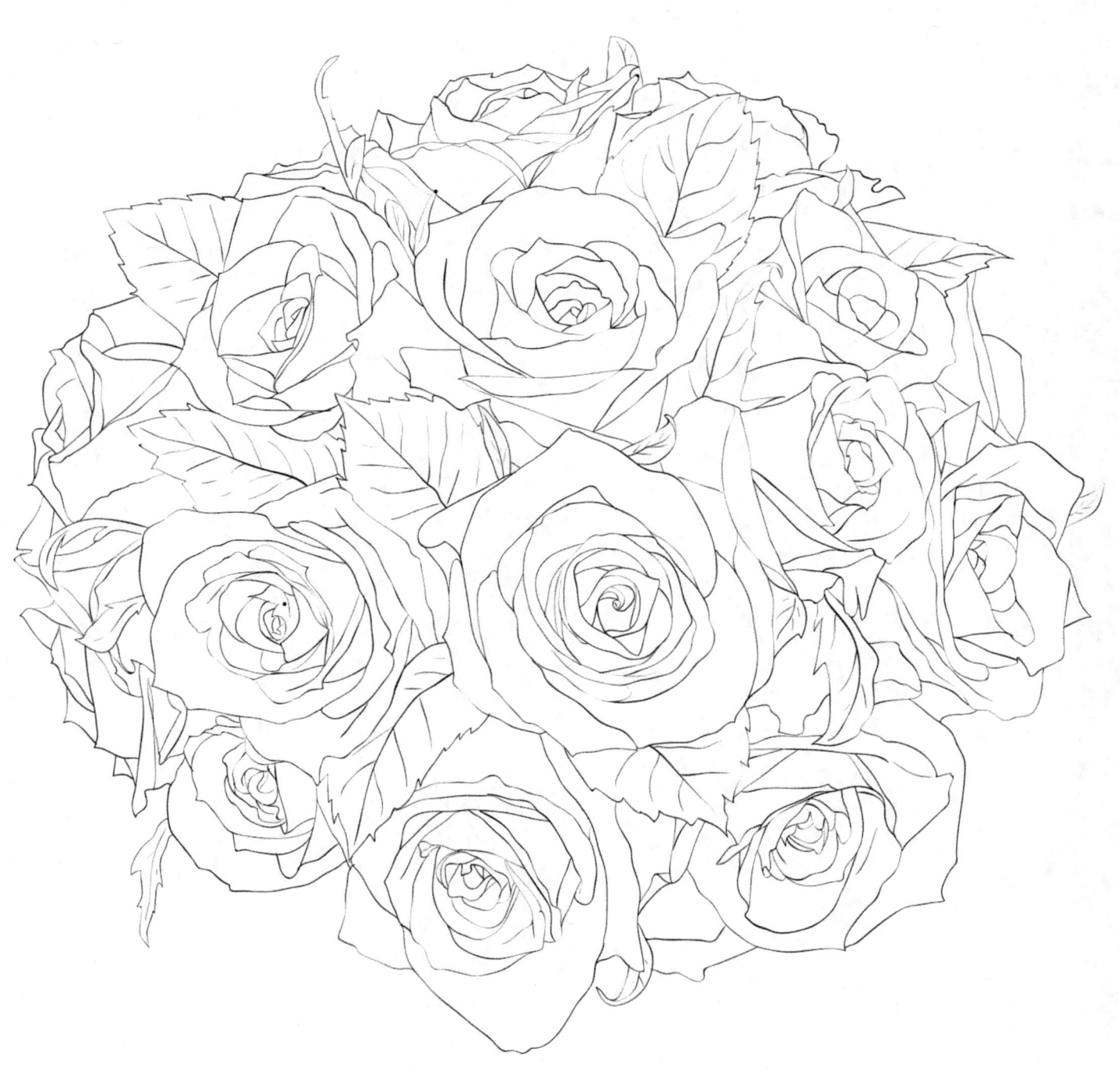

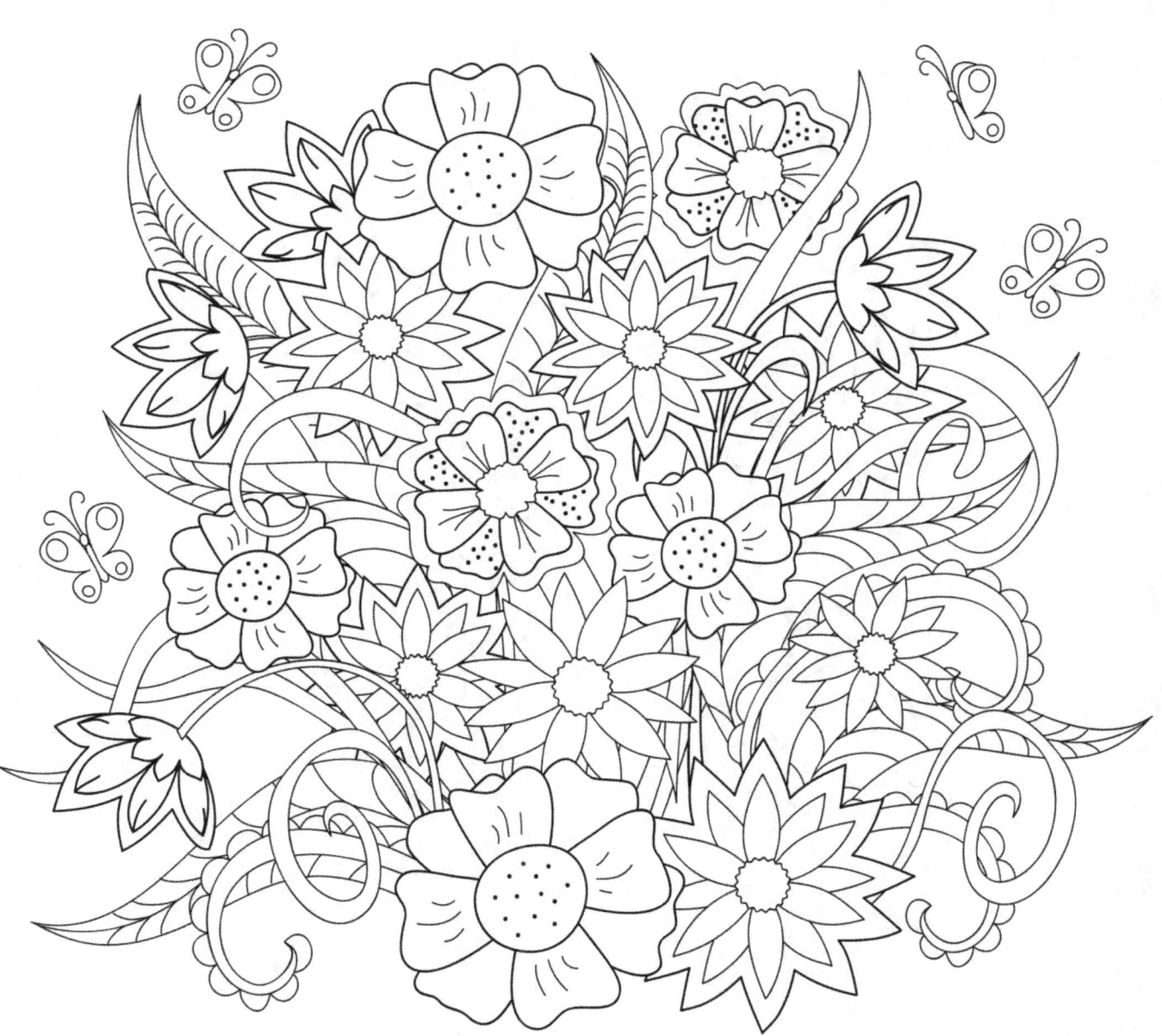

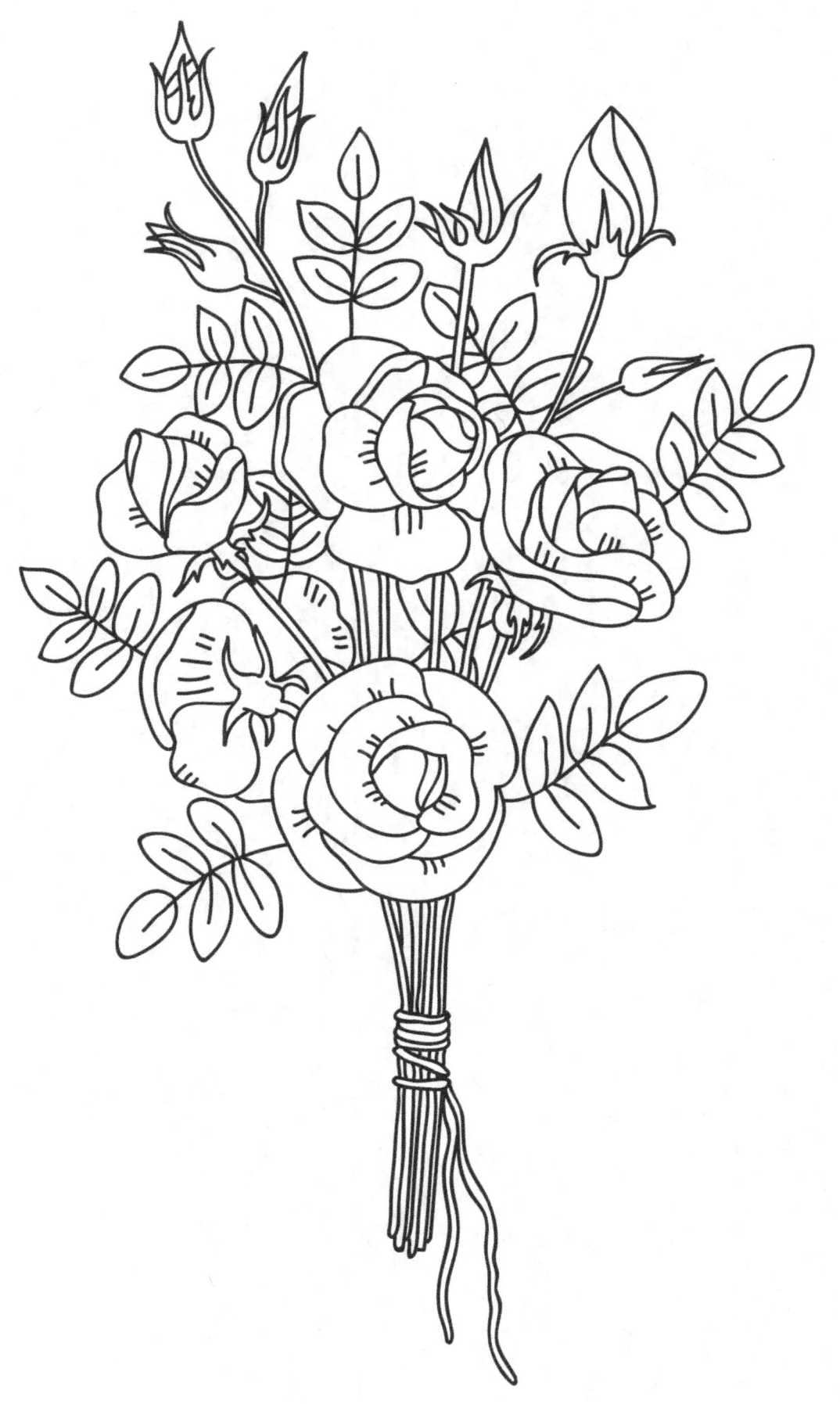

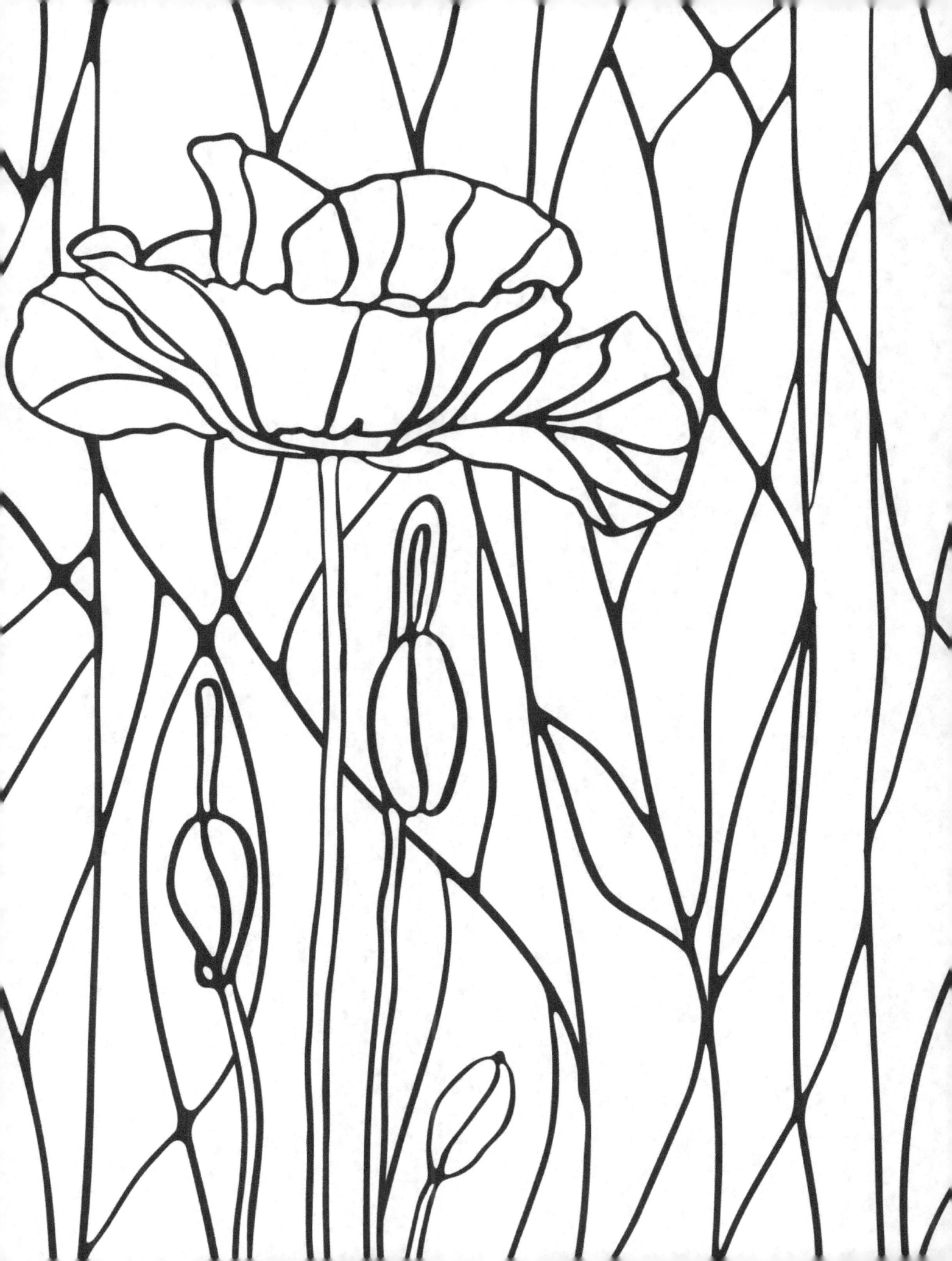

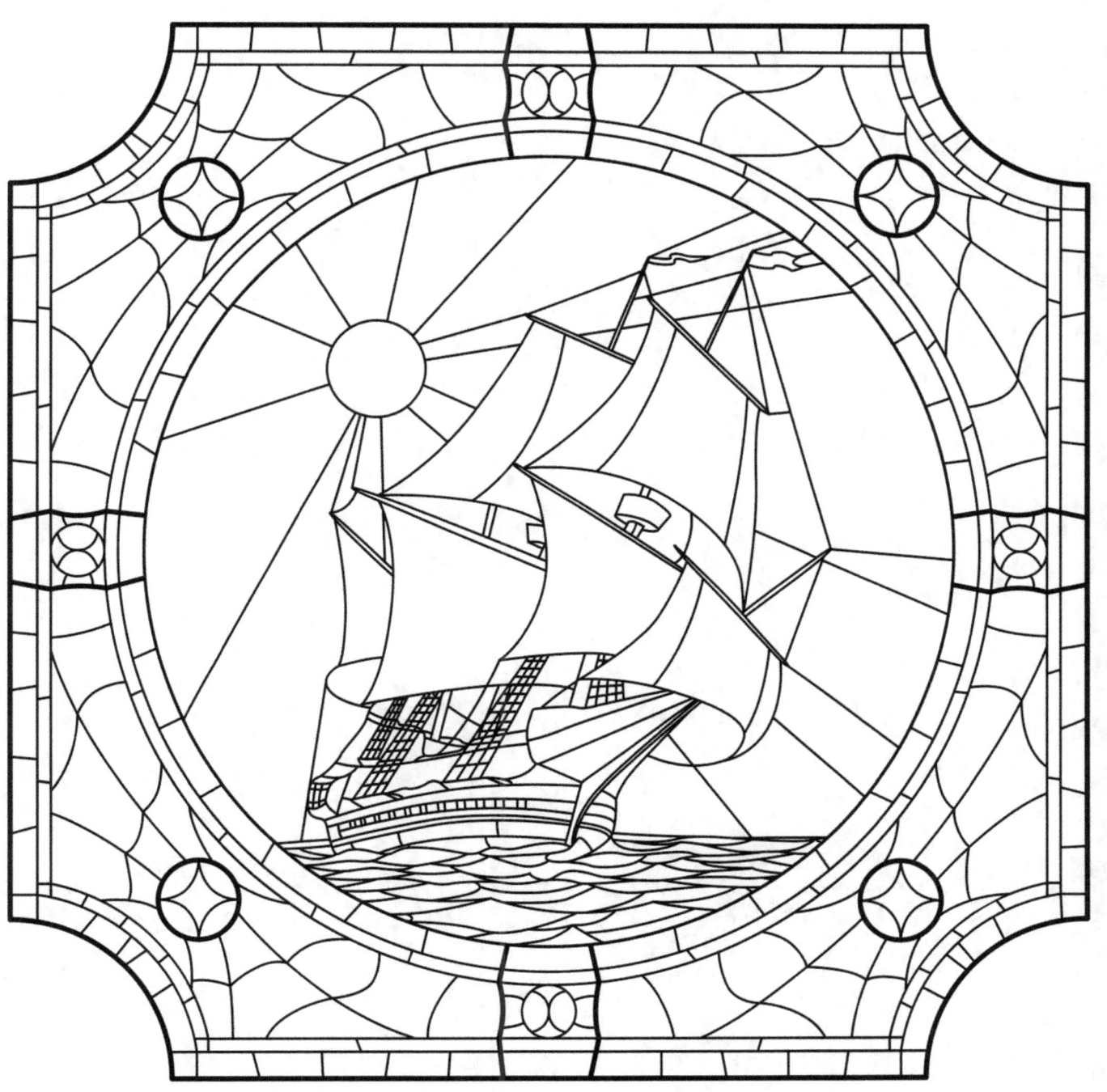

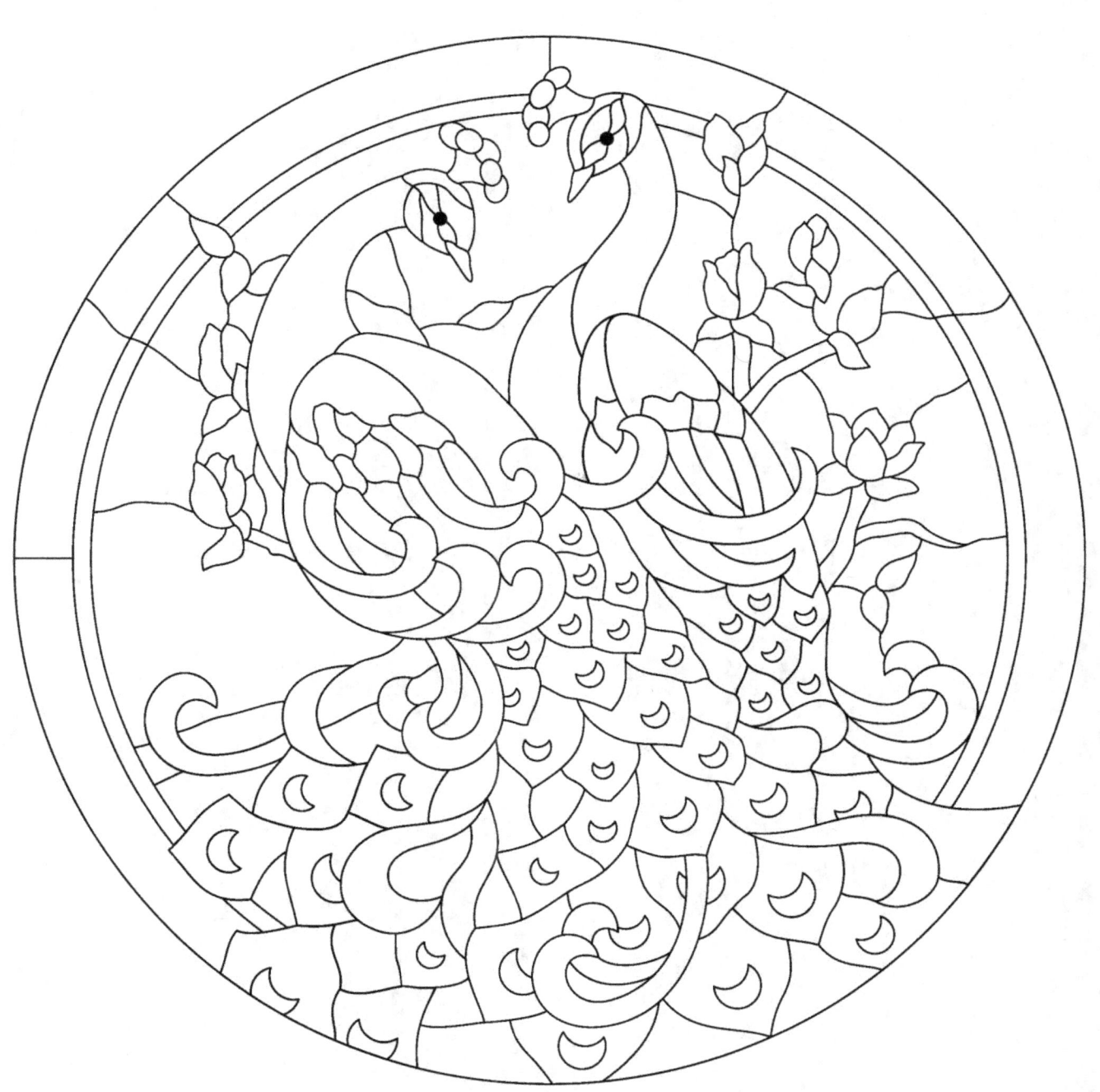

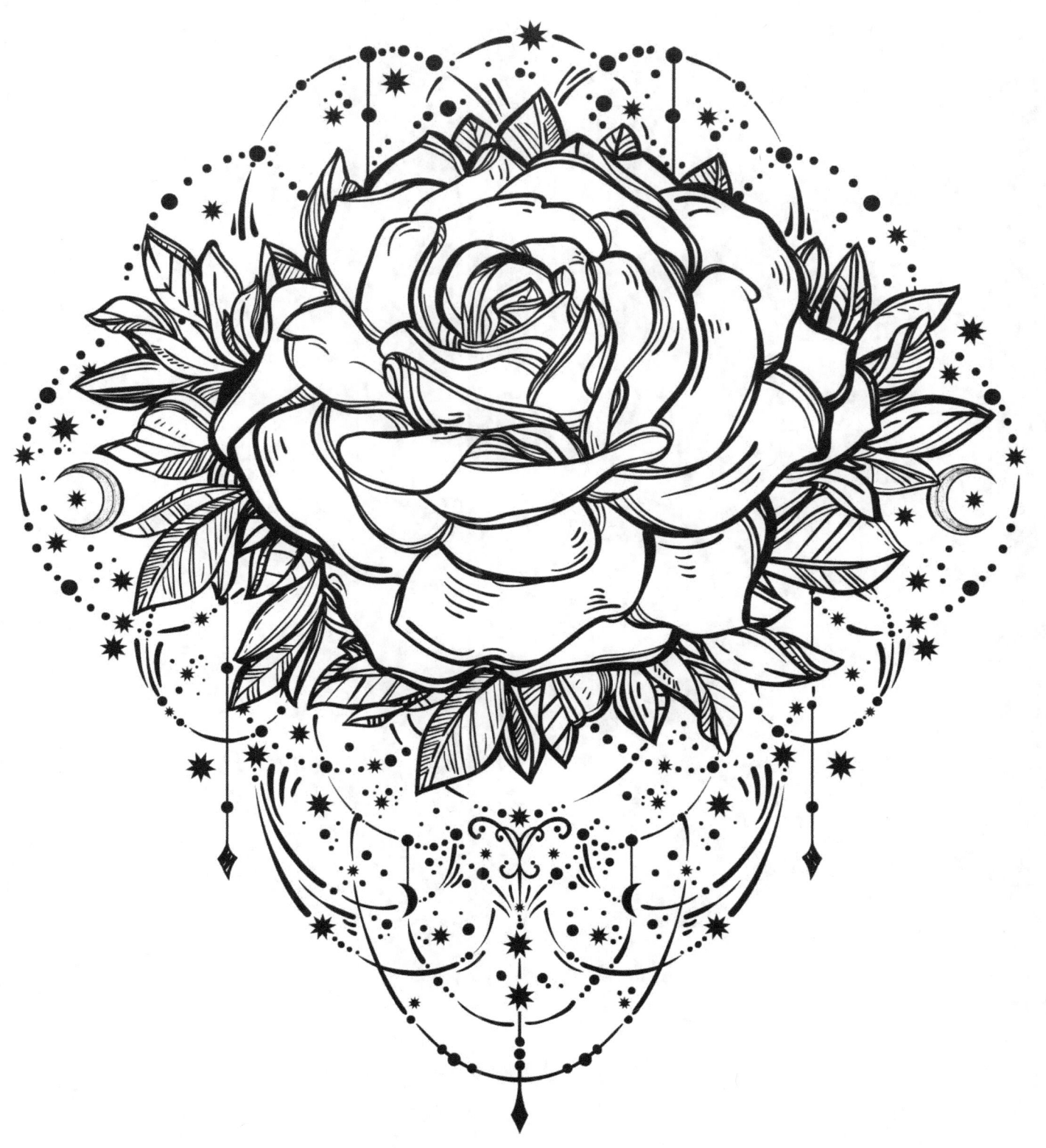

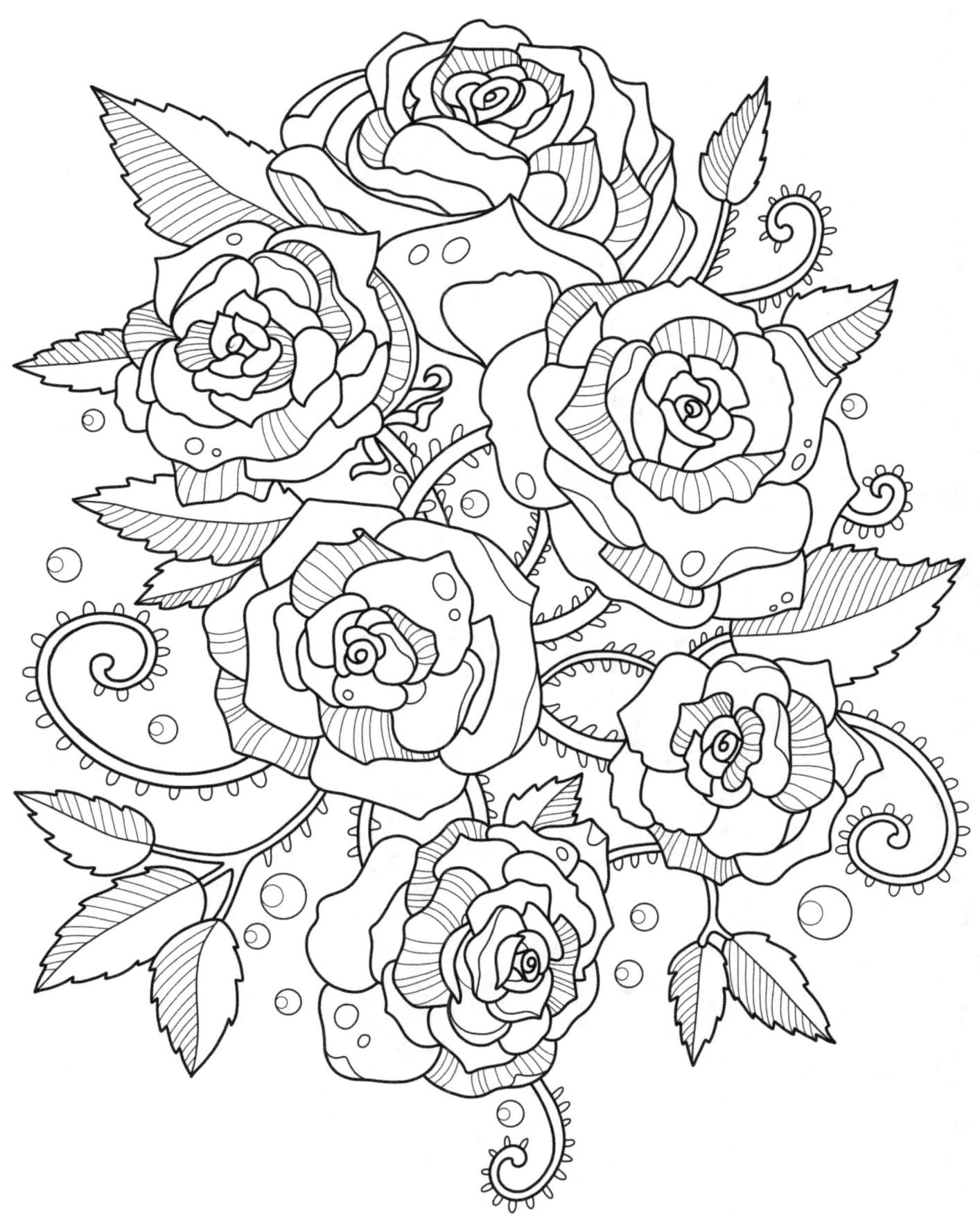

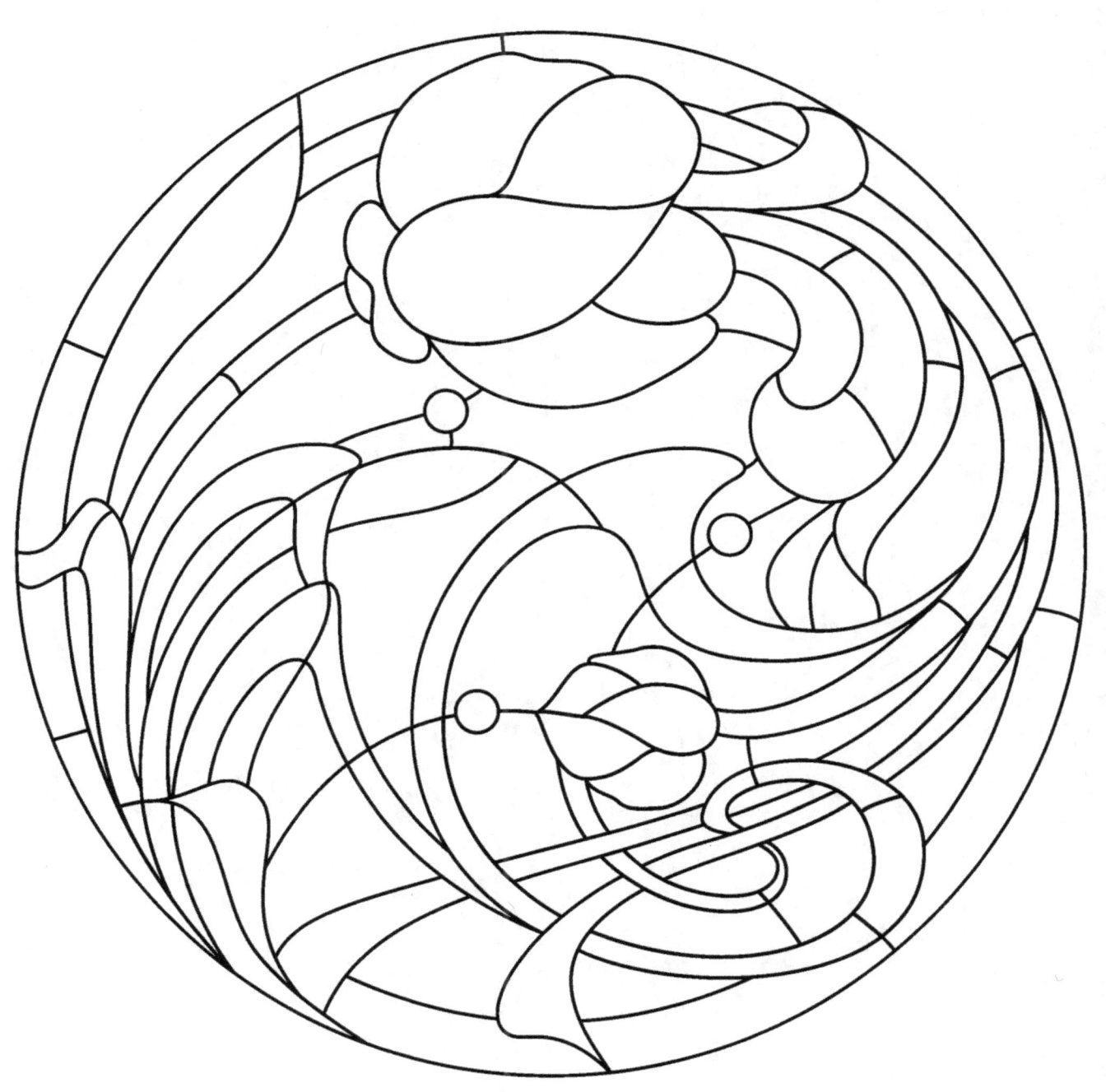

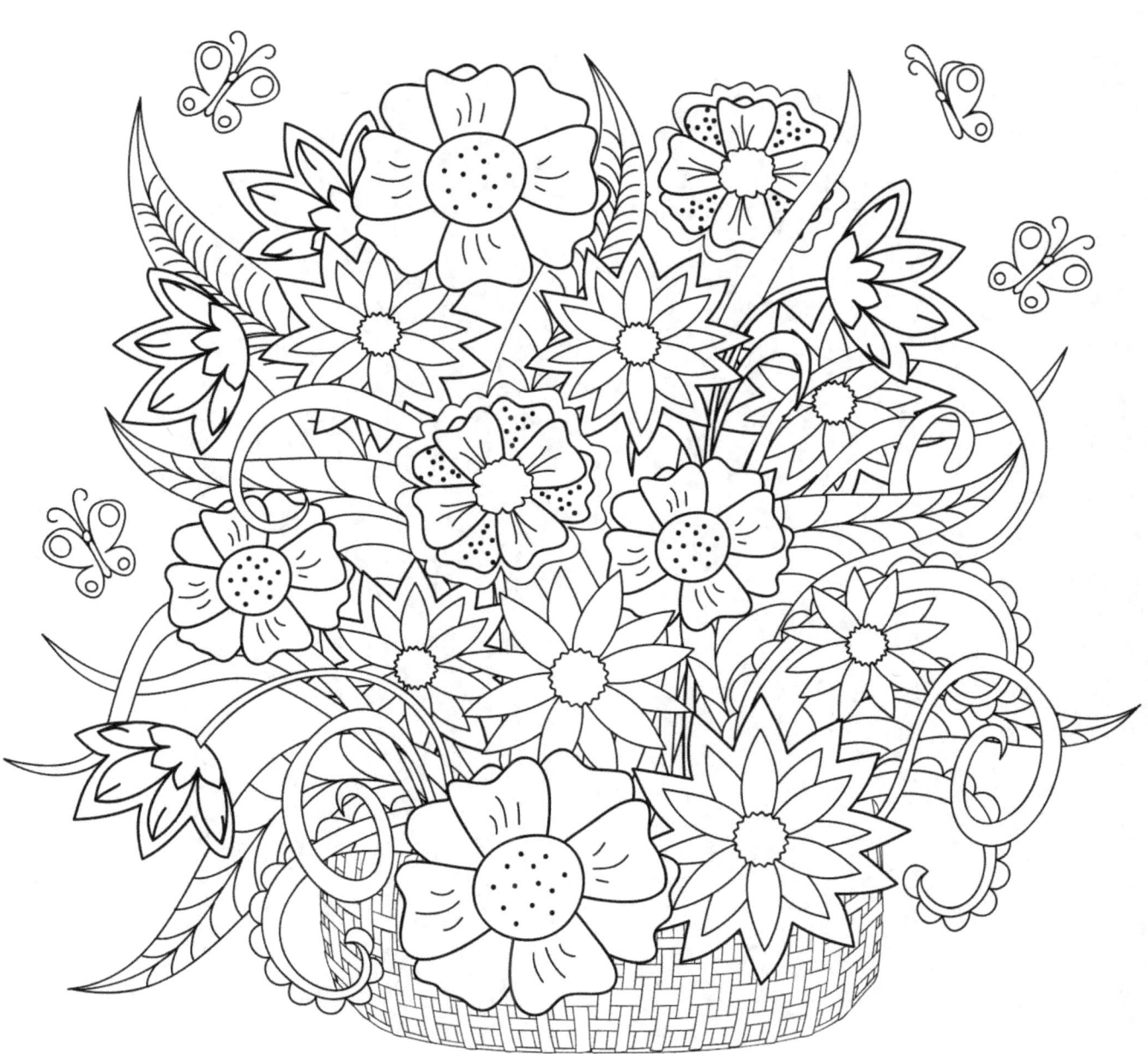

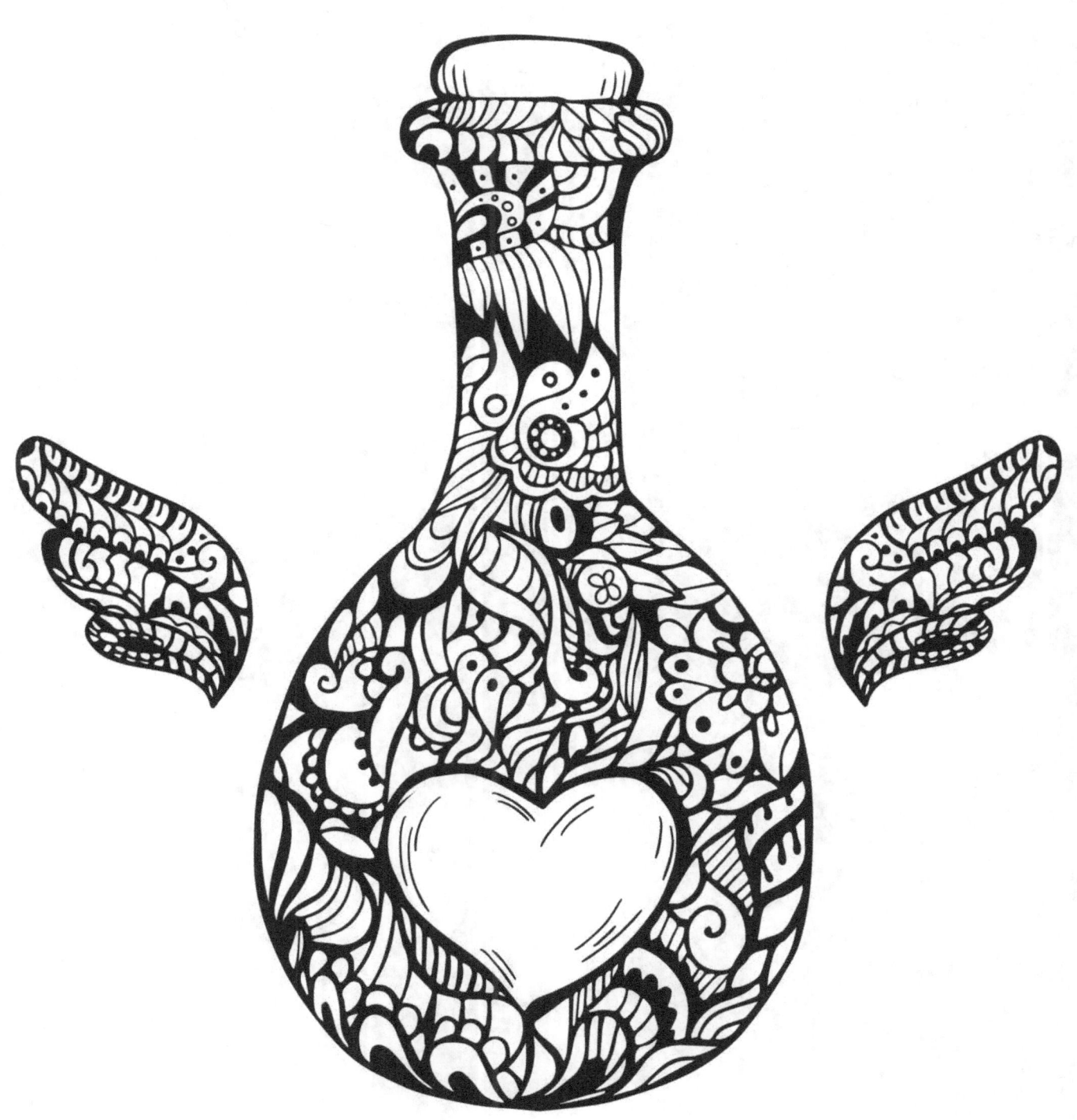

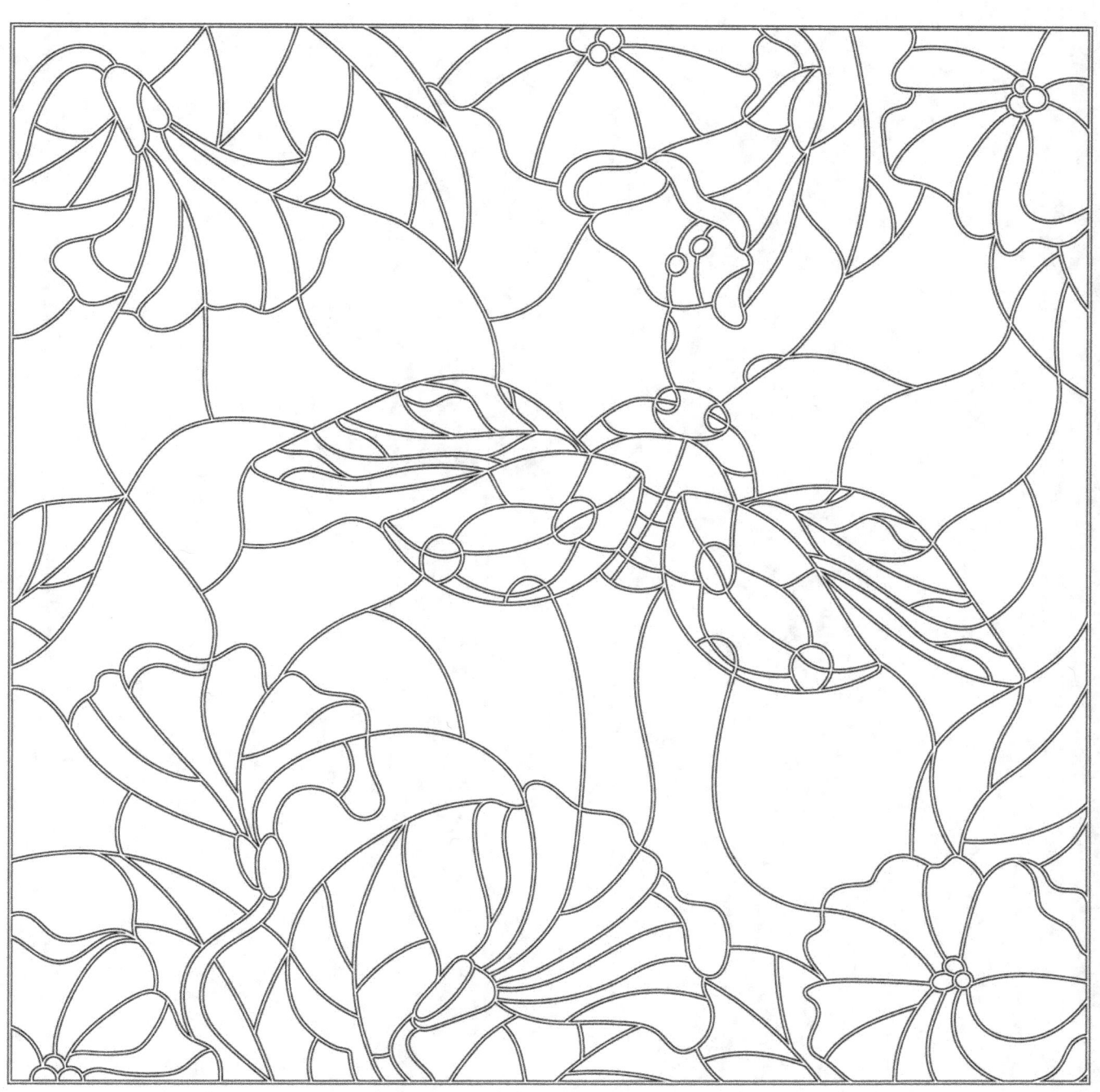

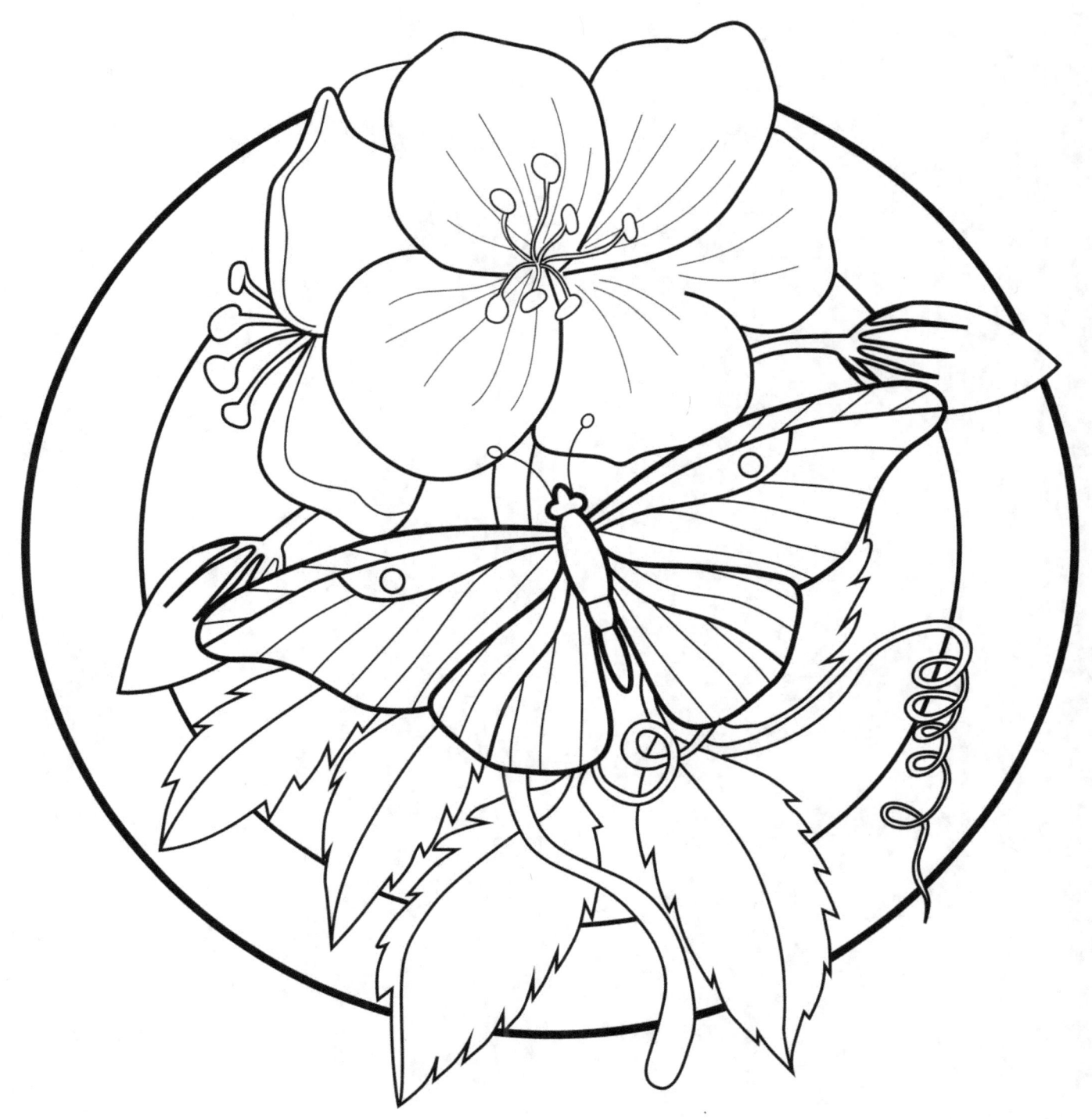

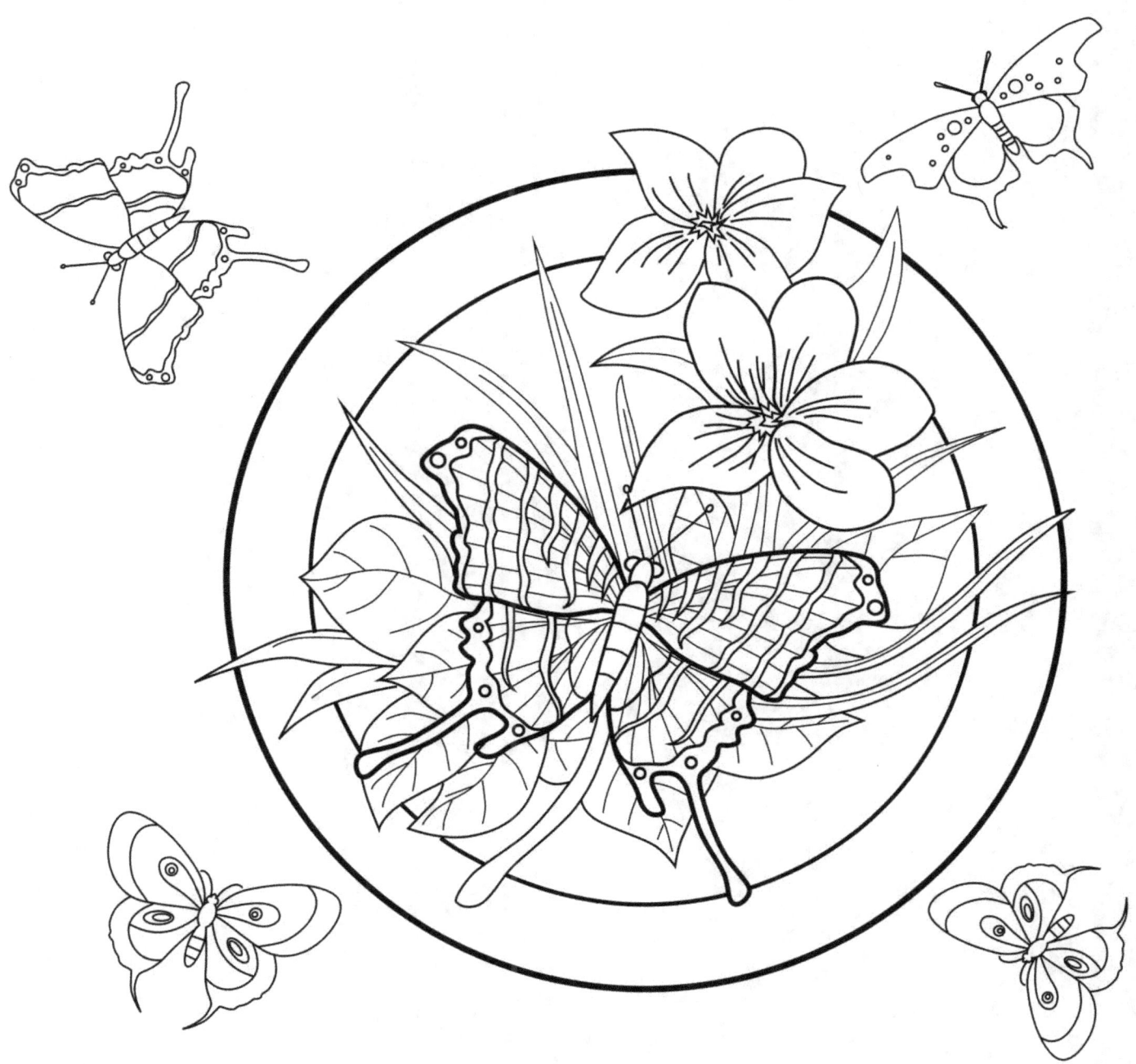

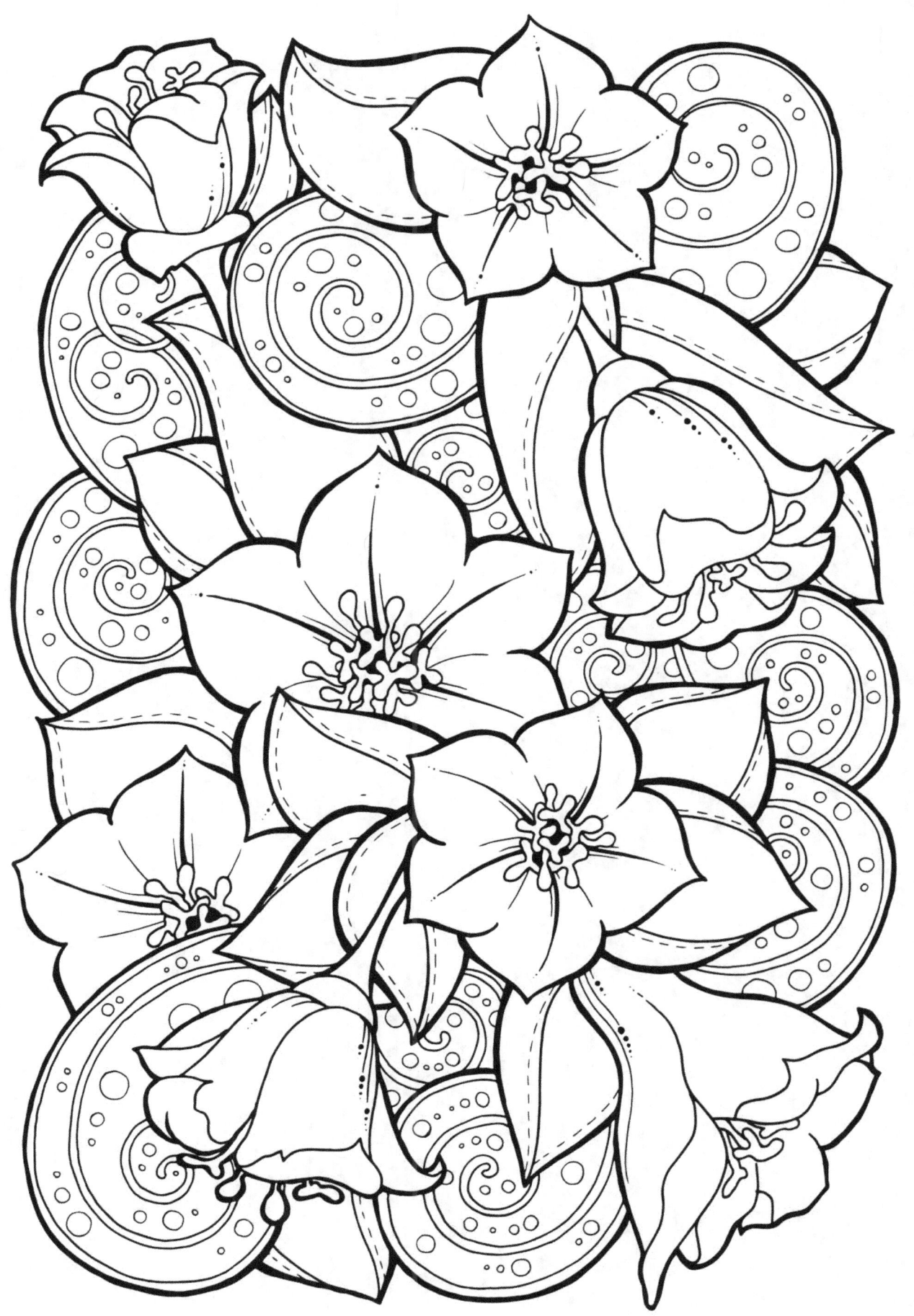

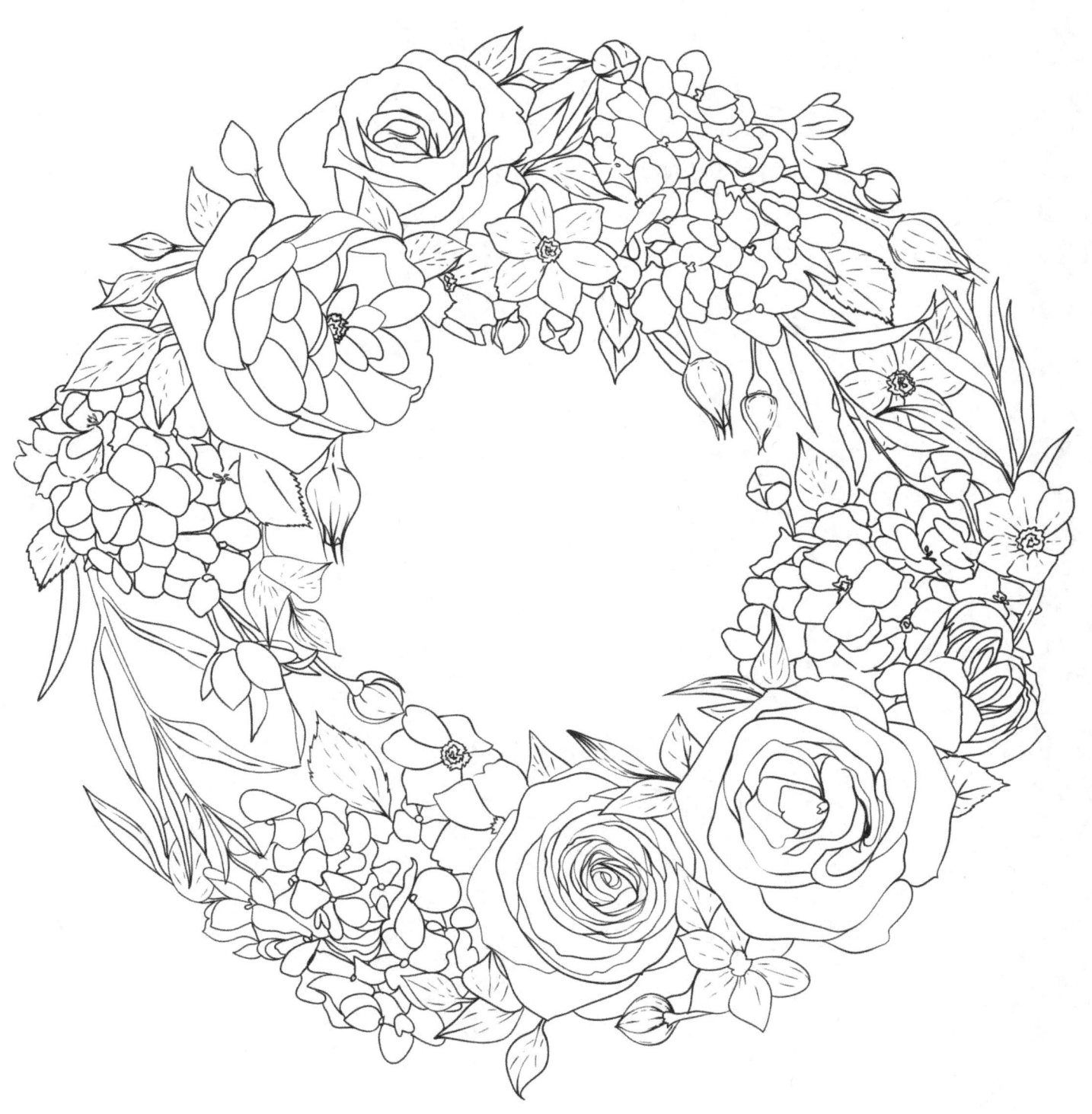

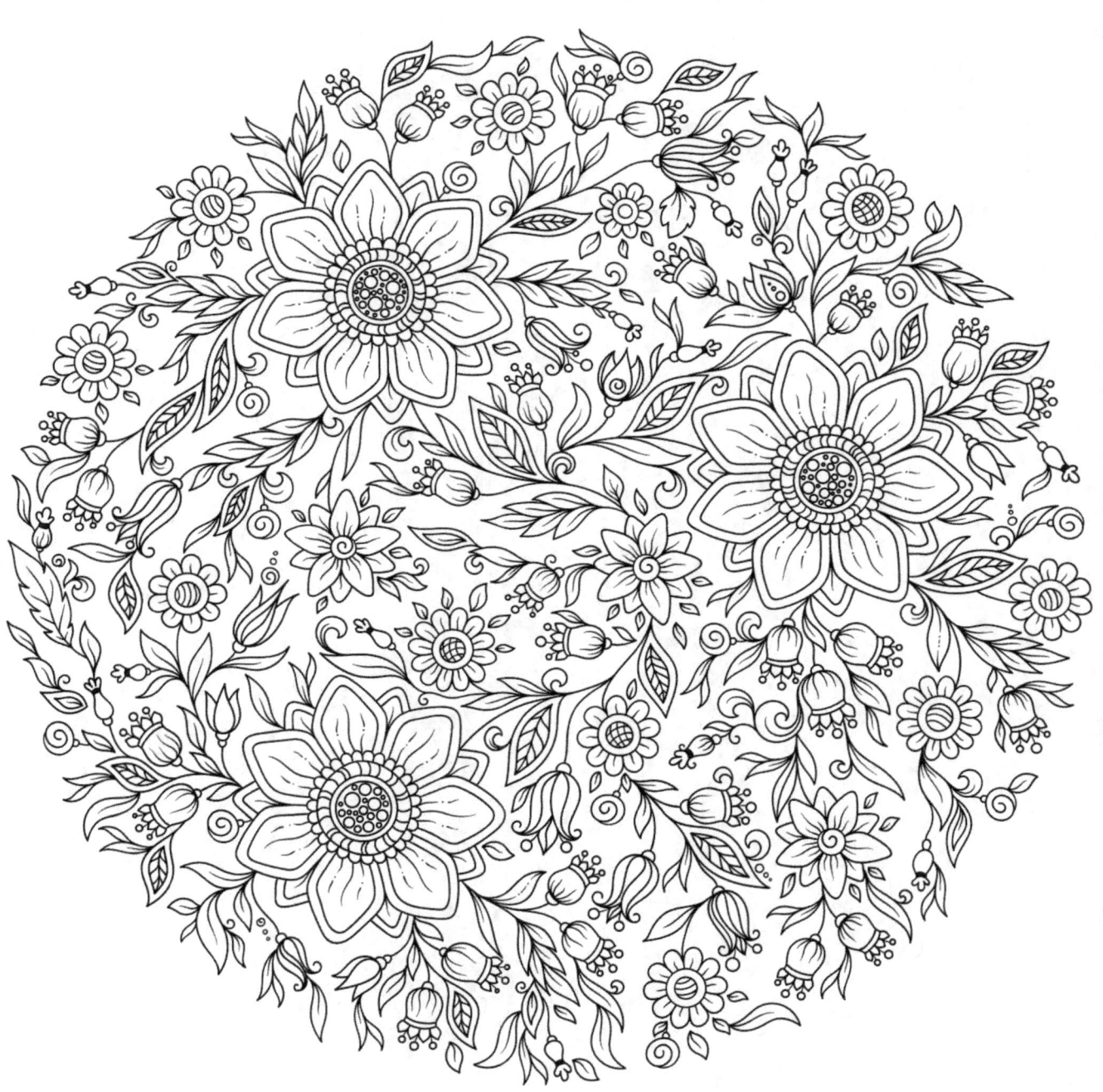

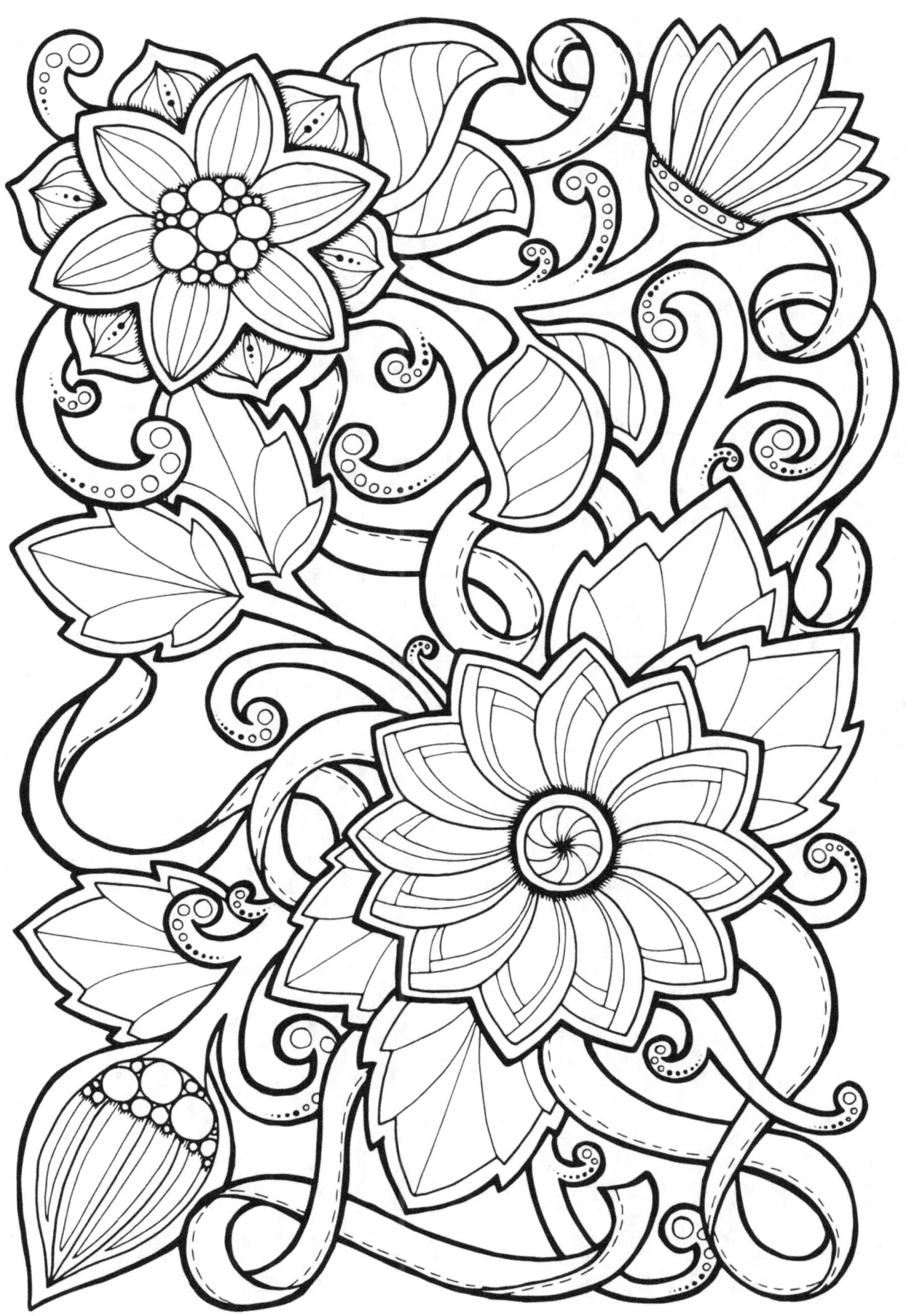

www.ingramcontent.com/pod-product-compliance
Lightning Source LLC
Chambersburg PA
CBHW081153280526
45787CB00008B/3313